Samuel and Nathaniel Buck's south-west prospect of Birmingham (1731). The Bucks took as their vantage point a position close to what is now the junction of Inge Street and Hurst Street, the future location of Court 15. Digbeth and Deritend is on the far right of the view. At its highest point (by St Philip's church) the town was 453 feet above sea level, a considerable challenge to the canal engineers a generation later. (See also rear endpaper.)

Living
Back-to-Back

Reconstruction drawing of the yard and back house in Court 15. The winding wooden staircase was the obvious solution to the lack of space in back-to-backs, but brought its own hazards, especially in the absence of a hand-rail. The drawing shows the interiors of the blind-back houses facing onto Hurst Street. Drawing: B. Byron.

Living
Back-to-Back

Chris Upton

Phillimore

2005

Published by
PHILLIMORE & CO. LTD
Shopwyke Manor Barn, Chichester, West Sussex, England

ISBN 1 86077 321 4

Printed and bound in Great Britain by
THE CROMWELL PRESS
Trowbridge, Wiltshire

Contents

List of Illustrations

Acknowledgements

Many thanks to my wife, Fiona Tait, for being the first critical reader of the manuscript; to Angela Quinby of Birmingham City Archives for advice on implications of the Data Protection Act; to the staff of the Birmingham Back to Backs and especially to Anna Russell and Laura Alden for countless visits; to Elizabeth Perkins of Birmingham Conservation Trust, on whose suggestion I wrote this book; to the Victorian Society for sponsoring my research; to the staff of Birmingham City Archives and Local Studies and History, and to Emma Hawthorne of the National Trust for advice and help with illustrations.

Illustrations are reproduced courtesy of the following: Birmingham City Archives, 66; Birmingham City Council, 1, 6, 75; Chris Upton, 2, 3, 76, 86; News Team International, 4, 82; Birmingham Post & Mail, 5, 8, 16, 28-31, 33, 34, 45-7, 51, 53-5, 62, 70-2, 83, 85, 88; Birmingham Library Services, 7, 9-12, 14, 17-19, 25, 26, 39, 44, 48, 50, 52, 56, 61, 65, 67, 68, 74, 77; Bournville Village Trust, *When We Build Again* (1941), 20, 41, 42, 81; Birmingham Open-Air Court Concerts Association annual report (1908), 23, 24; Ministry of Housing, 43; Birmingham COPEC Housing Improvement Society, 40, 80; Mr Peter Woodbridge, 73; John Bingham, 79, 87; Bette Brown, 84.

ONE

A Street in History

We live in many cities at the same time. There is the day-time city, full of shopping and traffic, with its gentle, predictable arc of opening and cashing-up and closing. Then there is the city at night, noisier and younger and much more volatile. But there are at least two others we inhabit too. There is the modern city of plate-glass and cashpoints. Above and behind it lies the city of the past, the back catalogue of an earlier era, not yet redeveloped and re-packaged, and upper storeys beyond the reach of plate-glass and neon.

In the centre of Birmingham there is a street that wears all of these faces. During the day Hurst Street is only half-awake; few shoppers venture this far, for ambitious shopkeepers have long since decamped to more profitable locations. The Cypriot-owned cafe is the last resort of those who still prefer tea to cappuccino, and bacon butties to baguettes. Across the road Mr Egg dispenses calorie-rich cures for hangovers.

But at night Hurst Street puts on better clothes or sometimes takes them off entirely. The Hippodrome opens its doors to the theatre crowd; the night-club doormen come out on sentry duty; the pubs compete with the clubs for volume of sound; and the taxis whirl round on an endless loop. The smell of eggs and bacon is replaced by Thai green curry and tandoori chicken. There are noisy queues at the taxi ranks, at the club doors, the cashpoints and the bars.

So where is the past in all this present? Listen and you can faintly hear it. Gertrude Falkenstein is pulling down the shutters of her shop. It is a winter evening in 1947. Mrs Falkenstein sells kosher meat to the Jewish people of the street, of whom there are many. Her shop is not the only kosher butcher's in Hurst Street—Abraham Blumenthal has one as well. Nor is she the only Gertrude in Hurst Street; Gertrude Tobias has a tailor's shop across the road. The locals call them Gertrudes 1 and 2. Life is hard for Gertrude 1; she has only taken over the shop in the last year and is still building up her clientele. But if times are hard for her, Gertrude 2 faces a tougher task by far. In Hurst Street every other shop seems to belong to a tailor. Hurst Street is the material world. Partly this is because tailoring has always been a Jewish speciality, together with watch repairs and jewellery-making, but there is the Hippodrome effect too. The theatre always needs costumes taking in or taking out, and the stars need a little dry-cleaning before the evening show. Not that haute couture is restricted to them. Every Saturday night Birmingham's young men pile into Harry Cohen's tailoring shop. In an upstairs room they sit around in their shirt tails while Harry presses their trousers down below. Only with the return of their trousers, creased as sharp as a razor, can the evening properly begin.

The sounds of 1947 fade away and earlier voices come through, fainter still. Two boys in caps are reading a poster outside the Tivoli Theatre. It is August 1900. The Tivoli calls itself a theatre, but it's really a kind of permanent circus, inferred by the attention-seeking spire on the roof, a cross between Blackpool Tower and a minaret. In fact, only one of the lads is reading, because the other has trouble with his words, and the poster is full of 'them foreign ones'. The poster tells of a woman called Orbasany and her performing cockatoos, and someone called DeMarce, who has a troupe of baboons and ponies. Exotic names are essential in this business: even the girls on the trapeze are called Trentonovi, although one of the lads swears they come from Small Heath. The two spectators drift gloomily away, knowing that a sixpenny seat in the gallery is beyond their means. They do not even bother to read the small print at the foot of the poster. It asks patrons of the Tivoli to inform the management of any offensive remark made by an artiste, or 'act of incivility on the part of any member of the staff'. The manager—Harry Calver—is rather proud of the wording here. He hopes it will cover him in case of riotous assembly. Birmingham theatres could get very uncivil indeed, and the city's notorious licensing justices did not take kindly to obscenity. They would be scrutinising the behaviour of the baboons particularly closely.

Fainter still, we can hear a voice from the 1820s.

> Before our door where I was born stood, on the opposite side, a considerable clump of well-grown trees, amid which was a hatter's working shop. On the adjacent corner of Hurst Street stood the Fox Tavern, as it stands now; but then the sign had been newly painted by a one-armed, short, quick-stepping, nervous-faced, dapper artist; and a very wonderful fox it seemed to me … Below the Fox Tavern was a 'Green'; at the bottom was a garden belonging to a house with a gateway, where one of my father's sisters lived. The garden fence was not a dead wall, but a low, wood paling, through which children could see the flowers in the garden. From the end of Inge Street the trees of the parsonage ground made a small wood before us, and apparently in their midst, but really beyond them, arose the spire of the 'Old Church', as we called St Martin's. On summer afternoons and moonlight nights the church spire, rising above the nestling trees, presented an aspect of a verdant village church in the midst of the busy workshop town. Down through the

'Green' the way led to Lady Well Walk, where more gardens lay, and the well was wide, clear and deep.

The speaker is George Jacob Holyoake, describing (after the lapse of 60 years) the street where he grew up. In later life Holyoake became a Socialist—before the word was common parlance—and a Secularist. Indeed, he was the last person imprisoned in Britain for being an atheist. His are the oldest eyes through which we can see something of an earlier Hurst Street. There are a thousand other voices, fading into the distant past, but we cannot catch their words. They are lost to us.

The sounds we can hear in Hurst Street echo those of other streets in Birmingham, and countless more in every town and city. And what we cannot hear we can reconstruct, using rates books and trade directories, census returns and building plans, maps and panoramas. But one thing makes this street special, and one place conjoins the past and the present in a way we could not have hoped for. At the corner of Hurst Street and Inge Street, facing what is now the Hippodrome and what was the Tivoli before it, stands a unique collection of houses. Earlier maps have a rather reductive name for it: they simply call it 'Court 15, Inge Street'.

For close on 200 years Court 15 has stood still, while history has ebbed and flowed around it. It has been home to perhaps 3,000 people, until in the 1960s legislation meant that it could be called home no longer and after that only the shopkeepers remained. It was in 2002 that the last occupant—George Saunders the tailor—pulled down his shutters for the final time. It was ironic that, after two centuries of Jewish tailoring in the street, the last man to ply the trade there hailed from the Caribbean.

What is it that makes Court 15 so special? For one thing it represents one of the last survivors of what was once the commonest form of housing in the Midlands and north of England. For the whole of the 19th century the back-to-back court was the most economic and practical solution to working-class housing. South from Leeds and Liverpool through Derby and Nottingham to the Black Country and Birmingham, courts spread through the inner cities, occupying every vacant lot or redundant back garden. By the First World War, 40 years after it had stopped building them, Birmingham still had 43,000 such houses, accommodating more than 200,000 people. In Leeds they continued to erect them as the Second World War approached, and they still live in them today. The estate agents, with their astute grasp of the English language, now call them 'single aspect houses'.

For two thirds of the working population of Yorkshire, South Lancashire and the Midlands, the back-to-back court circumscribed their lives. They were born there; they lived and died there, not always in the same court but often in an identical one a few streets away. Vast numbers of us have a parent or a grandparent who occupied one, families who pre-date the drift into the suburbs and the distant estates. Court 15 is therefore a tangible, physical link to a communal past, and its survival is as remarkable as it was unplanned. There were once so many such courts that no one considered their preservation until it was almost too late.

Indeed, so complete has been the expunging of back-to-backs from our urban landscape that the term itself probably needs a brief explanation. Like the terraced house that steadily replaced it, the back-to-back house was a 19th-century response to a specific housing need. Unlike the terrace it was only one room deep, with a single entrance either from the street or from an inner yard. Such houses were of two or three storeys, sometimes with a cellar underneath. In contemporary parlance they called them 'one-up and one-down' or 'two-up and one-down'. The ground floor served as an all-purpose space for living, combining the functions of living-room, kitchen, bathroom and dining-room, at a time when such functions overlapped entirely. The upper floor or floors were used as bedrooms, often divided by flimsy panelling to separate parents from children, or tenant from lodger. Cellars were generally only employed as a coal-hole, though in the poorer parts of Liverpool and Manchester they were lived in.

As such the back-to-back was not significantly different from the worker's or labourer's cottage of the countryside, and in all likelihood that is its origin. What made the urban version distinctive was the arrangement. As the name suggests, the back-to-back shared a spine wall with another house facing in the opposite direction, and the most common pattern is of a row of houses fronting the street, with a back row facing into an inner courtyard. The houses facing the street were generally considered superior to those behind, and the rent was adjusted to fit this fact. As the Rev. Charles Joseph told the Artisans' Dwellings Enquiry in Birmingham in 1884:

> It is an indisputable fact that, all other things being equal, the drunken man lives in the low-rented and squalid back-house, while the sober man lives in the more decent habitation at the front.

A trifle sweeping, perhaps, but undoubtedly reflecting the prevalent social values.

The arrangement of the court meant that the average house was hemmed in on three sides by other houses. Of course, this necessitated an alleyway to give access to the rear yard and to the back houses. In some towns the format did not fully develop. The one-room cottage might be only a blind-back, shut off by a windowless wall to the rear, or a single row of cottages shared an enclosed court. Such houses were no better ventilated or more sanitary than the back-to-backs, but did not attract quite the same degree of Victorian opprobrium.

This pattern was infinitely variable in accordance with the shape or confines of the site. One court was overlooked by a factory at the side or the rear; another shared a high partition wall with an adjoining court. One court might have as few as four houses in it, and another as many as twenty; one court might house only a handful of people; another could accommodate a hundred. The area bordered by Inge Street, Essex Street, Hurst Street and Bromsgrove Street, for example, contains courts with as many as 22 and as few as nine houses. These variations, the relative space in the court and the pressure on the services, were often reflected in the rental value of the properties and an unspoken pecking-order among the residents. The court at the corner of Inge Street and Hurst Street was probably considered to be superior to many exactly because it occupied a corner site, and the fact that only three of its houses faced inwards. As we will see, the landlord or his agent who fixed the rent took account of this fact.

The way each court was numbered for rental or postal purposes varied too. The earliest rating maps or censuses will tend to number the courts consecutively along a street, and the houses in sequence within each court: 1 house, 4 Court; 2 House, 4 Court etc. Earlier still the court might even by named after the landowner or tenant who built it. By the 20th century, however, enough courts were being demolished to disrupt the numerical sequence and to demand an alternative system of counting, whereby the back houses are numbered with reference to the ones that fronted the street: 1 back of 52 High Street. 2 Back of 53 etc. These are the kind of addresses indelibly printed upon the memories of many who lived through the 1920s and 1930s.

Not that this pattern of building was universal. The enthusiasm of builders and property developers for back-to-backs did not spread to every town. The middle of Birmingham was filled with them, but the centre of Wolverhampton had none. There were back-to-backs in Derby and Nottingham, but none in Burton-on-Trent; Worcester and Coventry had them, but not so Dudley and Walsall. Yet all these towns experienced a similar population explosion in the late 18th and early 19th centuries. However, these regional and local distinctions are more technical than real. All of the industrial towns of the Midlands and the North had court houses, and though the people in them might not share a party wall with another house to the rear, they certainly did share a court, along with the services that it provided.

The courtyard itself had a multitude of functions, although these varied over time. In the yard were the water tap, the washing-line, the wash-house, the toilets and the dustbins. It was a place for the children to play (although they usually preferred the street, where there was a wider clientele) and in warm weather to bath. There were sometimes workshops in it and the occasional fenced-off, but often infringed, garden. Our modern divisions between private and public space were here subverted by a notion, strange to us today, of communal territory. The yard itself was the great leveller, and any theoretical superiority felt by those at the front of the court was immediately undermined by the trip down the alley to the water-closet. The word 'privy' seems strangely inappropriate to what was actually the case.

Even within this simple arrangement of shared privies and party-walls there were considerable variations. In Leeds and Hull, towns with large numbers of back-to-backs, the houses were arranged in long rows, interspersed with service areas. In Morley and Huddersfield and some other Yorkshire towns many back-to-backs were built in blocks of four, allowing each house to have two external walls. Dr L.W. Darra Mair, whose investigation of mortality rates in back-to-backs in 1909 effectively condemned them to death, was not himself averse to this arrangement. It did, at the very least, allow for windows—and therefore through ventilation—on two sides.

The back-to-back was probably the most flexible and varied form of housing this country has ever seen, certainly compared with the carbon-copy terracing, council semi-detacheds and flats that followed. The houses were cheap and affordable, relatively inexpensive to heat and infinitely adaptable to the shape of plots. But for almost all of the 19th century they came with some very insanitary baggage. It was this, along with the perceived lack of privacy and dignity, that led to their demise.

Such a world is the territory of this book. It changes remarkably little in the course of 150 years, chiefly because those who lived in the back-to-back courts were not economically able to alter their external circumstances very much. As a result, the range, the scrubbed table, the tin bath and the outside toilet offer a surprising physical continuity between the 1830s and the 1930s. In much the same way the courtyard rituals of birth and death, bath night and wash day, effortlessly span the generations. It is disposable and surplus income that allows us to widen the circumference of our lives, both in how we choose to live and where. Those who occupied the courts did not have such freedom, nor did they necessarily miss it either. There was, and probably still is, a trade-off between privacy and possessions and community, though the latter is rarely noticed until it is gone.

The back-to-back died a very slow death. Although outlawed by some local bye-laws (Birmingham discontinued them in 1876), there was no national ban until 1909, and the court remained remarkably flexible even in decline. Between 1902 and 1905 Birmingham took advantage of the 1890 Housing Act to open up

33 courts by demolishing one side in order to allow light and ventilation (those Victorian cure-alls) to penetrate the dark interiors. Later still—and the court in Inge Street is a good example of this—those that survived could provide temporary accommodation for families joining the long queue for a council house.

So let us take one last look at Court 15 before we turn it back into history. On 23 July 2004 the court was officially opened to the public by the National Trust. The fires were burning again in ranges last lit in the 1960s; the feral cats and pigeons that once roamed the cellars and the bedrooms had vanished, and

1 An aerial view of the court taken in 2000 before renovation had begun. At this date the Inge Street frontages were occupied by a taxi rank, a chip shop and a kebab house. The back properties, by this time connected by doors to the front, were mostly used for storage.

2 Hurst Street frontages in 2004, with the Hippodrome on the opposite corner of Inge Street and Smallbrook Queensway in the distance. The theatre opened as the Tower of Varieties and Circus in October 1899, and reopened as the Tivoli in the following year. This had been Birmingham's principal entertainment zone since Day's Crystal Palace Concert Hall (later the Empire Theatre) was established at the corner of Hurst Street and Smallbrook Street in 1862.

3 Entry to the past. National Trust visitors to the court still take the same route as its former residents, down the narrow passageway and into the yard. More than 100 people volunteered to be trained as guides before the court reopened, many of whom had lived in a back-to-back in their earlier life.

even the brickwork was looking better than it had for a hundred years. The considerable task of fund-raising and restoration, undertaken by Birmingham Conservation Trust, was complete. In the first three weeks of opening no fewer than 4,000 visitors passed through the court and the level of media interest in the project was unprecedented. For a building of little architectural merit, and no famous connections, the enthusiasm with which it was embraced is remarkable. Yet it was not entirely clear whether the old court had been re-claimed by the public or reversed into the cul-de-sac called heritage.

What the preservation of Court 15 shows more than anything is the distance we have travelled in what we call heritage. If you are in any doubt of this, imagine telling the Victorian residents of this court that their houses would one day be open to the public. The word heritage was not in their vocabulary, not because of any imperfection in their schooling, but because they were not troubled by continuities between their present and past. The 19th-century word, had they come across it at all, had connotations of legal inheritance or God-given reward. Its emergence as an industry, as a tourist attraction or a policy of preservation, comes considerably later.

And yet it was the Victorians who more than any previous generation created the gap in the dictionary—somewhere between hereafter and hesitation—into which heritage would fit. There were many different aspects to this Victorian rediscovery of tradition: the embracing of medieval Christianity and its architecture by Augustus Pugin, of a lost ideal of craftsmanship by William Morris, of a tradition of liberal resistance by the Whigs. Above all it was an embracing of an idea of England and of Englishness. The children who lived in Court 15 heard a little of this when they went to school, or at least from the mid-1870s when there was a school for them to go to. They heard of Alfred the Great and William Shakespeare, of Lord Nelson and Good Queen Bess. But as far as they knew they themselves stood outside history. The tide of the past carried palaces and cathedrals and grand houses in its wake; assuredly it did not flow down Hurst Street.

We have changed our mind about this. We know that history carries everyone with it, castles and courtyards, cats and kings, and what we care to preserve is often indiscriminate and random. The Victorians would not have understood this. But what is certainly the case is that the decision to protect and renovate this court of houses caught a public mood. When the campaign was launched in 2001 Birmingham Conservation Trust and the National Trust were buried under a deluge of letters and phone-calls. Some had memories to share of their life in a back-to-back, and I have borrowed extensively from them in Chapters 5 and 6 of this book. Others contained offers of help and donations of artefacts; family photographs poured in and copies of carefully researched family trees. Few of the letters related specifically to the families who lived in Court 15, but they were part of a communal memory of which Court 15 was the catalyst. It was everyone's history that was being protected.

Only one letter of all those received was disparaging about the project. Why, the writer asked, should anyone want to preserve such a discredited aspect of the past? It was, on reflection, quite a pertinent question, and one which, more than anything else, has led to this book. The answer has something to do with heritage and

4 National Trust project director, Richard Goodenough, assesses the work to be done in one of the bedrooms of the court. Although the building was in a parlous and dangerous state by 2001, enough of the original features had survived to allow accurate reconstruction. Refurnishing, however, required more of an imaginative leap.

5 Court 15 during building work in 2003. Birmingham Conservation Trust coordinated the fundraising effort to repair and conserve the court. £1 million came from the Heritage Lottery Fund and £350,000 from the European Regional Development Fund, but many individuals also contributed to the restoration project.

history and education and democracy and politics, but I'm still not entirely sure what.

But there is one strong reason why this tale deserves to be told. The question of how we house our population remains as big an issue (to coin a phrase) today as it did when Court 15 was completed in the 1830s. It is not perceived as a crisis any more than it was in the early 19th century, yet it is one, and the two contrary aspects of it are as real now as they were 200 years ago. On one side the cost of homes is growing far beyond the means of the next generation to buy one. This is especially true in the desirable parts of the countryside and in central London, but is increasingly the case in all our cities. Currently the cost of the average house is rising by £25,000 a year, and our overall housing stock is said to be around 30 per cent overvalued. Ironically a home in the inner city (most likely a loft apartment) is now at the top of the property ladder, whereas 100 or even 50 years ago it was decidedly at the bottom.

Yet it is estimated that 1.1 million children are still disadvantaged by poor housing, one in twenty families is living in conditions deemed unacceptable, and four persons per thousand are homeless. At the same time the quality of our social and council housing is continuing to deteriorate. In 1997 it was estimated that two million houses owned by local authorities and housing associations were sub-standard. A quarter of all our houses were built before the First World

War. A century ago government policy was to transfer the problem of poor housing from the private sector to local government, triggering a house building boom that matched, if not surpassed, that of the early 19th century. A century later the policy has turned exactly around, shifting the solution back towards the private sector. Which is or has been the more successful approach is for history to judge.

Finding solutions to all this is not easy. The government estimates that we need an additional 140,000 new houses a year, on top of the 180,000 already being built. This, at least, would steady the rise in house prices.

6 George Saunders in his tailor's shop, shortly before its closure. George occupied the final two of the Hurst Street frontages under the name 'Take 2'. Hugo Sanchez, who ran a designer clothes shop in the two adjacent properties (57-59 Hurst Street), was in fact Cliff Saunders, George's son.

But what to do with the deteriorating state of local authority housing? In many areas the 'Right to Buy' schemes (introduced after the 1980 Housing Act) mean that the local council no longer receives enough money in rent to meet its repair and maintenance costs. Current policy is to encourage the transfer of council houses from local authority to private not-for-profit trusts. But tenants from Wrexham to Camden have overwhelmingly voted against such a move.

In 200 years, it seems—despite considerable progress in issues of health and standards of living—housing is a problem we cannot get rid of. But how did we get here in the first place? How did we move from cottage to courtyard, and from countryside to conurbation? That is the subject of the next three chapters.

TWO

A Maximum of Rent for a Minimum of Outlay

Across the great cities of Victorian England the back-to-back held sway. From the valleys of South Wales to East Anglia, and from the textile centres of Lancashire and Yorkshire down to the industrial centres of Birmingham and Coventry, the back-to-back ruled, along with its constant companions, the courtyard and the alleyway. No one has yet compiled a total for the number of such houses, but the result would be vast. By the early 1860s Liverpool had 18,610 court houses; two-thirds of the population of Birmingham were living in them by the 1850s. In Leeds 70 per cent of all houses—numbering some 76,000—were back-to-back in 1920, and around three-quarters of the residents of Nottingham lived back-to-back in the 1840s. Similar statistics could be produced for Manchester and Bradford, Hinkley and Wolverhampton. The overall total may well have been half a million.

To these bald statistics can be added eye-witness accounts. The journalist, Richard Phillips, wrote of Nottingham in 1829:

> The courts contained an abundance of small tenements, let to many stockingers like this, and there being many families and even extra lodgers in all, swarmed with population. Maggots in carrion flesh, or mites in cheese, could not be huddled more closely together.

The Medical Officer of Health reported to the Privy Council about the crowded condition of Leeds in 1859:

> The principal streets are fewer than is common in other great towns and the interspaces between the principal roads are occupied by dense and often complicated congeries of ill-kept streets and courts, which have but seldom been adopted as highways by the municipal authority, and are in a very foul state.

In 1844 Friedrich Engels likewise described the tightly-packed heart of Salford: 'All Salford is built in courts or narrow lanes, so narrow that they remind me of the narrowest I have ever seen, in the little lanes of Genoa.' And when Hugh Miller, a Scottish visitor to England also in the mid-1840s, conjectured that the mediocre streets of Manchester 'had been built by contract within the last half-dozen years' he was not far wrong.

From such descriptions it is easy to believe that the whole country was filled with courts, but it was not. There were none in Scotland nor in the north-east of England, and hardly any south of a line drawn from Essex to Bristol. Even London, where experimentation with housing was taken to a fine art, did not have them. There are lines to be drawn in history too. No back-to-backs were built before the 1770s and none after 1900 except in Leeds, whose long engagement with them could not be broken off until the 1930s. And of course—the most indelible line of all—only a handful are still with us today. These oddities, geographical and historical, deserve some explanation.

The housing boom that began in the late 1700s and ran, with the occasional trough, throughout the 19th century was society's answer to a rapidly increasing population, predominantly in the cities. In the middle of the 18th century the population of England and Wales was relatively static at 5.7 million, but had risen to 8.7 million by 1801, the first truly reliable figure. There were a number of reasons for this explosion, but the growing success of the British economy was at the heart of it. Increasing prosperity allowed people to marry younger and, as a result, have more children. Over these fifty years the age at marriage dropped by two years in men and three in women, and mortality fell slightly too. One in nine of the population lived in London, but all the English towns were growing. Leicester, for example, doubled in size between 1750 and 1800, a growth more than matched by Liverpool and Manchester. Nor was life in the countryside stable either. Enclosure of land, new farming methods and the loss of tied properties were increasingly unravelling the age-old ties to the land. Farm servants were migrating the most, but even established families moved too, if only short distances. Such migration was commonest among people in their teens and early twenties.

The change in people's lives were but the surface ripples of great tidal shifts. In short, the British economy was becoming industrial. Although it was growing slower than on the Continent British trade was directed much more towards the market than to subsistence, and a larger proportion of the workforce was no longer employed on the land. A nation of shopkeepers, as well as one of workshop owners, was being born. By 1750 more workers were employed in industry, trade and commerce than in agriculture. Alongside the growth of commerce came what looked like the shrinkage of the country. Road improvements (in the form of turnpiking) were increasing both commercial and tourist traffic. In one week in the summer of 1759, for example, a total of 259 coaches, 491 wagons, 722 carts, 206 drays and more than 11,000 horses passed through one of the turnpike gates between Bristol and the Midlands.

7 23 Court, Park Street in 1904. The speed with which the back-to-back courts were erected meant that little effort was made to level the land, with the result that water ran along the gutters and into the lowest houses. As Cumming Walters noted of a court in Gosta Green in 1901: 'The yard slopes sharply down and the water collects at the bottom, and threatens to run in at the doors of the three opposite houses. If the water near the stopped-up drain is stirred, the stench is unbearable. Nor dare the people properly swill the yard, because the water cannot be got away.'

England's long-established trade in wool was now being overtaken by far more profitable products. Coal production doubled between 1750 and 1800, then increased twenty-fold in the 19th century. The production of pig-iron rose four-fold between 1740 and 1790, and four times again by 1810. In 1780 the national output of iron was less than that of France; by 1850 it was greater than the rest of the world put together. Raw cotton imports rose five-fold between 1780 and 1800, and thirty-fold in the 19th century. As the railway engineer, George Stephenson, commented in the middle of the 19th century:

> The strength of Britain lies in her iron and coal beds. The Lord
> Chancellor now sits on a bag of wool, but wool has long ceased to be
> the stable commodity of England. He ought rather to sit on a bag of
> coals, though it might not prove so comfortable a seat.

The growing number of industrial workers in coal, iron and cotton required increased food supplies, and agricultural production rose steeply to meet the demand. One hundred Enclosure Acts between 1760 and 1800 took over seven million acres, and new technology was on hand to increase yields even more. Cereal rotation (the four-course rotation of wheat, barley, clover, turnips), the seed-drill, selective breeding and use of better fodder (especially the turnip) all served to industrialise the land as irrevocably as the fly shuttle (1733), the spinning jenny

(1764), the water-frame (1769), the mule (1779) and the power-loom (1785) were changing cotton production. Wheat output rose by 225 per cent between 1750 and 1850, and the number of cattle brought to Smithfield Market rose by 220 per cent. The reorganisation must have worked: unlike France, England suffered no serious famine after 1700.

All of which suggests a country that was industrialising at breakneck speed. Quite what form this industrial revolution took depended on which part of the country one was in. In the West Riding of Yorkshire weaving replaced pastoral farming as the principal trade. Hosiery made rapid strides in the East Midlands; lace making in Bedfordshire and Buckinghamshire; pin making, nailing and all sorts of other metalwork in the West Midlands. Most had begun as secondary occupations (often involving the whole family) to supplement earnings from the land; now the rising industries began to demand dedicated and full-time workers, and they wanted them closer to hand.

But what was to be done with all these newly urbanised families? Future ages would find more radical solutions for population shifts such as this: planning a new town, perhaps, or augmenting the ever expanding suburbs. The 18th-century response was much less radical; you might call it (literally) a stop-gap solution. The answer was in-fill. Geographically the Georgian town had moved little beyond its ancient roots. Medieval walls or simply parish boundaries had confined the conurbation within its old limits, apart from the occasional sprawl of cottages along the main highway. But this did not mean that the inner-city lacked space; there were yards, often found behind inns, gardens in abundance, and in many towns folds, the legacy of the old wool trade. Eighteenth-century town plans show how spacious the town could still be, and where they do not exist, the property section of the local newspaper is proof enough. Take this advertisement from *Aris's Birmingham Gazette*, dated 5 December 1743:

> To be sold and entered upon at Lady Day next, a large messuage or dwelling house, situate in Temple Street, Birmingham, in the possession of Charles Magenis, containing twelve yards in the front, four rooms on a floor, sashed and fronted both to the street and garden, good cellaring and vaults, brew-house and stable with an entire garden walled, and the walls covered with fruit trees, the garden 12 yards wide, and 50 yards long from the front of the house, and extending 20 yards wide for 26 yards further, together with a pleasant terrace walk, and summer-house, with sashed windows and sashed doors ... and set at nine pounds and ten shillings per annum.

A property such as this offered considerable potential for the would-be purchaser. He could, of course, simply live in it, but the possibilities lay way

beyond this. For one thing the garden could be built over, with room for half a dozen small cottages; for another the house itself was ripe for conversion into two or more smaller dwellings. A home divided was a home increased in value. With a little judicious redevelopment a house and garden with a rent of less than £10 a year could quickly be worth ten times that amount.

Such radical conversion would today be subject to a lengthy planning process, but no such red tape tied up the property of the 18th and early 19th centuries. Where local government existed—and unincorporated towns such as Birmingham had little in the way of local control anyway—it did not have powers over the alteration of property. Here, as in most aspects of civic life, the free market ruled.

There were two main components in the development of a site such as the one in Temple Street described above, or three if we count the tenants who would shortly be moving into the new houses. Firstly there was the landowner himself. Although it might not be apparent on the surface, the freehold in towns was usually divided between a handful of substantial land-owners, whose power to change the face of urban areas was as great as their influence upon patterns of farming in the countryside. In another generation this would be a contentious political issue. In 1879 the radical American economist, Henry George, published his book *Progress and Poverty*, which advocated a single tax on land irrespective of what was on it. In the lecture tour that followed George railed against the power of the landlords. At Birmingham Town Hall on 23 January 1884 he thundered against one landowner in particular. His words were printed verbatim in the local press, including the reactions of his audience.

> You have a great landlord named Lord Calthorpe *(hisses and applause)*, a man, I believe, who has never come to this town *(hear hear)*, yet who draws from it yearly an enormous sum. For what? For land that existed before he was—before any of us were, before the race was—for land that will exist long after he and we will be dead and gone. It comes necessarily from the work of the men of Birmingham. (*Applause.*) You have another family, I am told, who own land in the centre of the town, land that has gone up within some years past 12,000 per cent. Who made it go up? It was not what this family did that did not live in Birmingham. It was what you, the men of Birmingham, did!

Henry George's opinions deeply influenced Joseph Chamberlain when he was drawing up his Improvement Scheme in the 1870s. But the reality of the situation in the 18th century and still, it should be said, today, is that the freehold of many central areas remained and remains in the hands of a small number of owners.

8 One side of the back-to-back court was often closed off by the high wall of a factory or of an adjoining court. By the 1960s such Victorian brickwork was often in a poor state of repair. In 1965 these housewives in Hanley Street, Aston, protested about the dangerous condition of what they called 'Death Trap Alley No. 2.' The prospect of wash day being interrupted by the collapse of a 30-foot wall was not an appealing one.

The central issue was, how did these landowners intend to exploit their position? By the middle of the 18th century the pressure to build was proving irresistible, and the comparative values of the built and un-built environment showed the way forward. By the 1780s farmland fetched around £2 an acre, land in parcels for grazing averaged £4, allotments yielded £16 an acre, while land let for building was worth £24 an acre. In 1746 a House of Lords committee was told by witnesses for the Colmore Estate Bill that building on the estate would increase its value from 30s (£1.50) an acre to £15. The sales pitch in the local press begins to reflect this change, and the references in advertisements to 'mature fruit trees and commodious summer houses' give way to descriptions of gardens 'capable of conversion to dwelling-houses'.

The key decision for the landowner and his agent, therefore, was not whether to redevelop, but when. Land values did not increase at a uniform rate and releasing too much land onto the market at one time could easily depress prices. So could an economic slump, such as those of the later 1770s (coinciding with the American War of Independence) and the mid-1790s (at the time of war with France). It was, as always, a delicate balance between supply and demand. Typically, however, land was released in small parcels, often no more than a few hundred square yards in size, and such sales might be staggered over several years.

9 10 Court, Cheapside, in 1905. This cheerful little court belies the impression that life in the back-to-backs was necessarily gloomy and oppressive. That said, it's unlikely that the potted plants so proudly displayed on a number of window-sills would have leafed so well in the end house, under the forbidding shadow of a 30-foot wall. The court in question had 10 houses in it, and its next-door neighbour was a chandelier and lamp manufactory.

10 Two girls entertain themselves with an old chair in Bagot Street *c.*1904. Bizarrely, this court has been opened up at the front, but the three WCs still stand with their back to the main road. All three toilets have, it seems, been converted to water-closets, but only one has been supplied with a modern pedestal. By the 20th century many such outside toilets were no longer leaking into the yard, but were taking in the rain instead.

11 33-35 Cheapside in 1904. A rare image showing both the street and a glimpse into the hidden world that lay behind the street frontages. The cast-iron plate over the entry, giving the number of the back court, is typical and one such plate survived on Court 15. The name 'Pettifer buildings' recalls the name of the original builder of the court.

The press advertisements have more to tell us too. The announcement of the leasing of land at Deritend in May 1788, for example, ensures potential clients that this was to be no rural backwater:

> The public are requested to take notice that the street called Bordesley Street is intended to be carried all the way to Bordesley, and there unite with the London roads, forming a street of a mile in length, and of sufficient breadth to admit of an uninterrupted passage for all carriages travelling between this place and the metropolis; the several other streets intended to communicate therewith are also marked out, as well as land in the centre of the same for a chapel and burial ground, forming together a plan for a beautiful hamlet.

It was, as this notice makes clear, also the landowner's duty to stake out a street pattern in advance, at least where there was not one already in existence. Land without a street frontage was of little use to anyone.

Which brings us to the developers themselves. With property values rising as steeply as they were, buying or leasing a small plot and redeveloping it represented a secure and tempting investment for the middling classes. Even taking into account the cost of a mortgage and the lease, such investment could easily yield 10 per cent profit a year, and later still the lease—along with the occupiers—could be re-sold at a considerable mark-up. Apart from shares in a canal company and the short-lived South Sea Bubble, property represented the best investment on the 18th-century market.

Evidence from across the country suggests that it was small businessmen and traders who leapt onto this bandwagon. As Nassau Senior somewhat superciliously remarked after a visit to Ancoates in Lancashire: 'A carpenter and a bricklayer club together to buy a patch of ground and cover it with what they call houses.' But the pattern allowed for large-scale speculation too. In Leeds a pocketbook maker called Richard Kendall developed a block of 64 cottages at the beginning of the 19th century, and even his efforts were dwarfed by those of Richard Paley, who built 275 houses in the East Ward, and sold land for 290 more. The range of speculators is large, but especially it was those already involved in the building trade who invested. Such individuals might well already be dealers in building materials, such as bricks or timber, which would help to keep down the overall cost of development. Joseph Willmore, the man who leased the plot on Inge Street from the Gooch Estate, was himself a carpenter. The men who took on the leases of the other plots on Hurst Street included a spectacle maker, a silversmith and a cabinet maker.

But the purchaser was unlikely to do the building himself; this job would be contracted out to others. As such he was at the mercy of the market in terms

12 A court in William Street in 1905. Birmingham Corporation made a photographic survey of all 'slum properties' at this time, creating a unique visual archive of life in the courts. So confined were the interiors that most residents preferred to sit outside whenever possible. The fox terrier, seen at the far end of the yard, was a more than useful rat deterrent. Interesting also is the contrast between the three-storey houses and the two-storey ones. This must have been a warm day—windows are rarely seen as open as this.

BACK-TO-BACK HOUSES

A TYPICAL COURT OF 14 BACK-TO-BACK HOUSES

The three general plans are shown in the block adjoining the street;
the block at the back of the court; and in the inset.

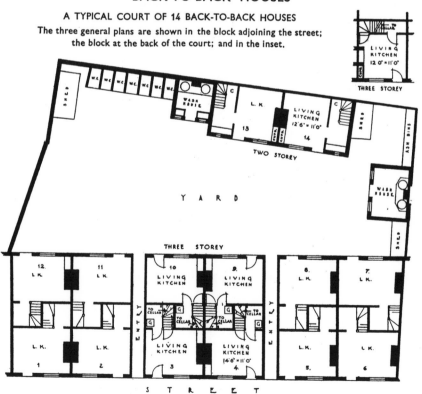

13 Plan of a typical back-to-back court, showing the dimension of rooms. The court has 14 houses and a double entry. The proportion of WCs to families is easy to see: seven water-closets to 14 houses. There are two brewhouses, each with two coppers. At the date in 1941 this plan was made Birmingham still had 38,000 such houses.

of wages and materials; the shrewdest investor would build when demand and inflation were flat, but rising. The best arrangement of all was if building materials could be had locally. An advertisement in *Aris's Gazette* in January 1788 for land in Ashted, a little to the north of Birmingham, makes this very point:

> The extensive beds of good clay and sand upon the premises (in addition to the desirable situation) will afford the tenants great advantages in the opportunity of getting bricks and sand upon the spot, on very easy terms ...

And if that was not alluring enough, the estate agent went on to note that the rates here (being in the parish of Aston) were only two-thirds those of Birmingham.

In secure possession of his plot, the new owner was now in a position to build, and there were a number of financial considerations that induced him to build small. For one thing the rent from a number of small houses would certainly exceed the rent from one larger one. For another, properties rated under £10 per annum were not subject to poor rates, a cost that the owner would have to bear himself. Finally—and here we are led inevitably towards the back-to-back—two houses sharing the same roof and the same spine wall—not to mention the same toilets—would obviously cost less to build. To skimp on size, build on insecure foundations and cut down on materials represented the best way to ensure a return on one's capital. A report of the Bradford Building and Improvement Committee in 1864 labelled the economies 'a maximum of rent for a minimum of outlay'. It was socially disastrous, but financially understandable.

Again we have contemporary accounts to back this up. In the 18th century houses are usually categorised according to the number of rooms on each floor, the largest town houses being typically of four rooms per storey. Such a house could be built in the 1790s for around £400. But for the person renting such a property luxury did not come cheap. In 1787 the engineer, James Watt, gave advice to a Dutch merchant considering relocating to England. Watt tells him:

> I pay £28 rent for the house I live in and have two parlours and five bedrooms, kitchen and brewhouse and laundry in a separate building. Parlours one 15 feet by 18 feet, one 14 feet square with closets off it. Rent £20, Poor Rate £8. House and Windows Tax £6 16s. Church levies £2 2d. Highway levies 14s.

All this before considering the servants' tax and the cost of their livery. Only a man with a monopoly on steam-engines could venture into this realm. Lower down the social scale, a two-room house, consisting of parlour and kitchen on the ground floor and bedrooms above, would cost about half that amount. A court house would typically cost between £40 and £60 to build, depending upon its size and how close it was to its neighbours. But having a 'footprint' of only one room, it was possible to squeeze as many as 60 houses on each acre of land.

Such a house would bring in rent of perhaps £5 and £6 a year, but that sum would always be rising. The rate at which the capital was paid off may well have determined how quickly the buyer moved on. Chalklin estimates that 80 per cent of property remained in the builder's hands for at least five years, and 50 per cent was still in his possession after twenty years. The court in Inge Street was still in the hands of the family who built it until the 1850s, half a century after building work had begun.

These then were the economic impulses that determined the way that our Victorian cities grew. Given such substantial returns, it was no wonder that William Hutton could write of Birmingham's property boom: 'The itch for building is predominant; we dip our fingers into mortar almost as soon as into business.' The growth of city centre living reflected, as it does today, both a social need and a fast buck. James Hole, whose *The Homes of the Working Classes* was published in 1866, was as aware as any of what was happening here. He writes of the craze for back-to-backs:

> Hundreds of them are being run up by mere building speculators,
> who build them not for permanent investment, but for immediate sale,
> and hence put as little material and labour into them as they can.
> No effectual control or inspection exists to check such proceedings.

Such sentiments were echoed by R. Baker in his report on the condition of housing in Leeds in 1842:

> In periods of prosperity, no property is more valuable than what is
> called cottage property in towns; for the demand for labour enables the
> operatives to pay a high rent, which, for the most part, is collected weekly
> or quarterly, according to the character of the tenantry. Thus whole
> streets of houses have arisen in Leeds, in an inconceivably short space
> of time, and in many instances evidently for the sole end of speculation,
> without regard to the absolute want of the tenants.

But whatever reputation for poverty, deprivation and ill health the back-to-back would be winning by the later 19th century, we must be careful not to transfer such attitudes backwards. In Nottingham, for example, the number of houses—predominantly back-to-back—grew from just over 3,000 in 1790 to 12,600 in 1841. But the building boom allowed the average number of occupants per house to shrink from 5.5 to 4.1. In Birmingham the number of houses rose

from 12,000 in 1801 to more than 27,000 in 1841, but here too the instances of overcrowding or multi-occupancy dropped. Dr John Darwall gave the town of Birmingham a complete medical examination in 1828 and pronounced:

> ... the streets are, for the most part, wide and spacious, and the courts have, generally, large yards. Unlike Liverpool and Manchester, excepting that part of the town which is occupied by the Irish, it is rare to find more than one family in one house, and I know not any situation where cellars are occupied by dwellings.

The back-to-back house offered working-class families the social ideal of middle England: a home of their own. No matter that they had to share a wash-house and a toilet, and the whole family might well share the same bedroom, the sense of exclusivity remained. And what was often called the 'urban cottage'

14 Back houses in 5 Court, Barford Street, in 1904, overshadowed by a factory. Such an arrangement made sense in the 18th and early 19th centuries, when work and home were in close proximity. But the introduction of heavy plant was not good for the brickwork or the plaster. It was said that many houses rattled continuously when the machinery was operating.

was no better and no worse than many had enjoyed in their previous lives in the countryside. Indeed, it could seem remarkably similar. Information given to the Children's Employment Commission in 1841 about living conditions in Birmingham could easily be describing a site in deepest Herefordshire:

> The courts vary in the number of houses, of which they contain from four to twenty, and most of these houses are three storeys high and built back-to-back. There is a wash house, an ash pit, and a privy at the end, or on one side of the court, and not infrequently one or more pigsties or heaps of manure.

As Dr Darwall notes, it was only in places such as Liverpool and Manchester, where a cellar underneath the back-to-back regularly accommodated another family—something like 20,000 people in Liverpool in the 1840s—that the standards were significantly compromised.

The earliest back-to-backs in Nottingham were erected in 1775, but by far the majority of court housing was constructed between the last decade of the 18th century and fourth decade of the 19th, a period of just 50 years. It was, as we have seen, a remarkably flexible form of housing, the number of properties determined by the shape and size of the plot, and the size of the plot probably pre-selected the kind of investor who would make use of it.

But not all such houses were built by the sort of private speculator described above. Once accepted as a standard form of working-class housing, the back-to-back begins to turn up everywhere, sometimes as much an instrument of philanthropy as a blank cheque. In West Yorkshire, for example, cottages were often built by mill-owners to ensure that their workers lived close to their place of work, and such enterprise can be paralleled by the 'double-houses' (a variation on the back-to-back), built in Ebbw Vale and Blaenavon for the mine workers. Edward Ackroyd's back-to-backs at Copley, near Halifax, are an early example, but not entirely typical, in that he supplied piped water. In Nottingham, though the proliferation of back-to-backs and blind-backs was not the result of a company policy, nevertheless the houses were both built and designed with stockingers and cotton spinners specifically in mind, with a shop or workshop in the attic above the chamber.

Most surprising of all, the very organisations we might have expected to eschew back-to-backs were themselves responsible for some of the earliest. The terminating building society was a club which allowed a small group of members to save on a regular basis, and as the funds accumulated each member in turn was allocated a house. Once each of the club members was housed the society was terminated. The first such clubs are to be found in the West Midlands in the 1770s, the earliest of all probably being Ketley's, founded in Birmingham in

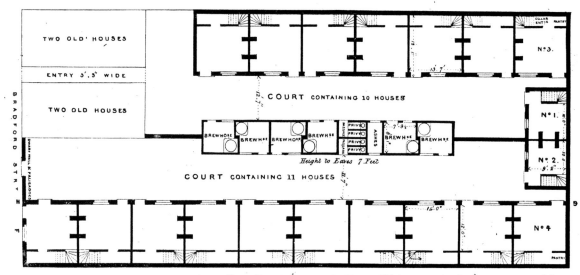

Houses N.ᵒˢ 1 & 2 are two stories, & are without cellars. Rental 2/- per week. Houses N.ᵒˢ 3 & 4 are let for 3/- per week. The whole of the other new houses, which as well as the houses 3 & 4, are three stories in height, and have all cellars, are let for 3/6 per week.

HEIGHTS
Ground Floor Rooms 7·8
First Floor   D.ᵒ   8.0
Second Floor D.ᵒ   7.2

about 1775. Such clubs demanded a sizeable financial commitment—between 4s and 6s a month or a fortnight and sometimes additional payments as well—and were therefore beyond the means of the lowest class. It's not surprising then to see that the members of the Amicable Society, which erected houses near Five Ways in Birmingham, included a silversmith, a timber merchant, two gentlemen, two pocketbook makers and three victuallers. For those ready and able to bear such outgoings a foot on the (independent) property ladder awaited them a few years down the line. Northwood's Building Society, formed in 1781, leased its land in 1785 and assigned its houses seven years later in 1792. By 1870 around 13,000 houses in Birmingham had been built in this way.

Such societies were certainly not averse to erecting back-to-backs and blind-backs. Indeed, M. W. Beresford argues that the earliest back-to-backs in Leeds, the standard-bearers of a veritable legion of courts, were built by one such society. These were on Union Street, and were erected by the Crackenthorpe Garden Building Society on land of that name in the late 1780s. Others, built by the Hill House Building Society, followed shortly afterwards on King Street and Queen Street. These houses could not have been especially well-appointed: they were the first to be pulled down by Leeds Corporation under the 1870 Improvement Act.

Thus, by a combination of shrewd investment, private speculation and growing demand the maps of our cities were re-drawn. It was not simply that

15 Ground plan of recently constructed courts in Bradford Street, from Edwin Chadwick's *Report on the Sanitary Condition of the Labouring Population of Great Britain* (1842). As in Inge Street, the new houses have been built behind already existing ones, but the courts have been cleverly constructed to allow even the brewhouses to be built back-to-back. Chadwick commented favourably on the arrangements here; nevertheless, there are only four privies to 21 properties.

more people were now living in them; more radical still was the nature of the new urban spaces that had been created. No longer was the street line a true guide to who lived where. There were now communities that lay out of sight, an outcast hinterland of mass housing invisible from the street and unpenetrated by those who did not live there. Half of these people now lived with their back to the outside world, as if the whole concept of the English town had been inverted, and the space turned inside-out. The yards they inhabited were neither private nor public, but a curious state in between. But most unsettling of all, at least to those who still believed in one nation under the Sun, there were now parts of town into which the middle classes did not venture, dark areas that did not concern them and which they knew nothing about.

It was this fear, intermixed with a distant curiosity, that eventually drove the legislators and the social reformers into the courts. Such feelings were still to the fore in 1884, when the Royal Commission on the Housing of the Working Classes called Joseph Chamberlain as an expert witness. The exchange went like this:

> Do you consider a system of building for the poor in courts is a satisfactory system of building?
>
> Yes, I think so, decidedly.
>
> You have never had brought under your notice any moral disadvantages arising from the isolation of people away from public opinion, and from the general eye of the world?
>
> No, I do not think it applies to courts which are properly lighted and ventilated, and which are all in connection with the main street.

The Royal Commission was not as confident as Joe about this. Nor was the Select Committee on the Health of Towns. As its report put it, somewhat patriarchically:

> … the wealthy and educated gradually withdraw themselves from these close and crowded communities; which thus stand more and more in need of some superintending paternal care.

By the middle of the 19th century paternal care, if that was what it was, was arriving by the coach-load.

THREE

Living at the Bottom of Wells

No age has collected statistics as avidly, and with such a sense of dread, as did the Victorians. The annual volumes of the National Statistical Society (begun in 1839) show that there were legions of determined individuals, as well as organisations, crunching numbers on a regular basis, and they brooded endlessly on disposable income, the price of potatoes, the mortality of amputation, the rate of inflation and the railway timetable.

What triggered the explosion of statistics is not easy to pin down, but one factor was undoubtedly the appearance in 1798 of a pamphlet entitled *Essay on the Principles of Population*, published anonymously, but in reality the work of the Surrey curate, Thomas Robert Malthus. The views of Malthus were not especially original, but they were here presented in a clear and chilling form. In his monograph Malthus argued (and backed up with examples from history) that the human population naturally grows faster than the available food supply, that is, unless natural checks, such as disease, war or malnutrition intervene. These, as it were, represented God's way of maintaining a healthy balance. Malthus

16 Roof-tops in Small Heath in 1977. The introduction of terraced housing from the 1870s onwards considerably improved both the life expectancy and status of the aspiring working classes. But in spite of the attempts by builders to provide a little (mass produced) decoration on the front, such ribbon development was often condemned as monotonous and dreary.

himself advocated voluntary action—'moral restraint' from marriage or the practice of birth control—to slow the rate of population growth.

Whatever the truth of the Malthusian theory the debate over it led to the first Census Act (1800), followed in the next year by the first census. Only with accurately compiled statistics—more accurate, at least, than those derived from parish registers—could argument be fully joined. The civil registration of births, deaths and marriages followed in 1837, and from that point onwards the collection of statistics became a major concern both of local and national government. We should add that Malthus may well have been influenced by Britain's profound economic crisis of the last years of the 18th century. Food shortages in 1795-6 approached famine proportions, and war with Revolutionary France led to massive unemployment. As a result the cost of Poor Law provision rose from £2 million in 1785 to £4 million in 1801. These statistics were as worrying as any.

The ten-yearly censuses provided for the first time largely accurate figures for the population of England and Wales during this period:

1801	9.2m	1861	20.0m
1811	10.2m	1871	22.7m
1821	12.0m	1881	26.0m
1831	13.9m	1891	29.0m
1841	15.9m	1901	36.1m
1851	17.9m		

Hidden behind this simple table were many more significant changes. The rate of population growth between 1811 and 1821, for example, was the highest ever recorded in the UK. Most important for us, perhaps, was the accelerated switch between rural and urban living. In 1801 around 26 per cent of the population lived in towns and cities, compared to 74 per cent in the country; by 1891 the figures had almost exactly reversed, to 28 per cent (rural) and 72 per cent (urban). The census also allowed these figures to be accurately allocated to the urban areas themselves. Manchester had grown from 75,000 (1801) to 303,000 (1851) and London from 959,000 (1801) to 2,362,000 (1851). Over the whole century the population of Birmingham rose from 60,882 (1801) to 522,204 (1901), though this did include some boundary changes.

Migrants were tumbling into the cities in unprecedented numbers, and there—in equally unprecedented numbers—they were dying. Again there were statistics from the Registrar General to prove the point, though it was the spin put upon them by the newly appointed Compiler of Abstracts, Dr William Farr, which made the point most powerfully. Farr's examination showed a rural death rate of 18.2 persons per thousand, compared with mortality in towns of 26.6 per thousand. Such figures become even more powerful when converted into more

human terms. In 1841 in Wolverhampton, for example, average life expectancy was just over 19 years; in Penkridge, the Staffordshire village to the north of the town, it was 37 years 9 months. Nor was Wolverhampton the biggest killer of its population. In Liverpool the life expectancy of a labourer was 15 years, while that of a professional person was 35 years.

It did not need the filing cabinets of a William Farr to recognise that death was organised geographically. As Henry Mayhew wrote in the *Morning Chronicle* in September 1849: 'Indeed, so well known are the localities of fever and disease that London would almost admit of being mapped out pathologically, and divided into its morbid districts and deadly cantons.' A generation after Mayhew, Charles Booth would do exactly this.

But it was not simply the rise in the urban population, it was what this brought in its wake that caused anxiety. From the 1820s onwards various bodies wrestled with what were seen as primarily urban problems. Pauperism, criminality, improvidence, sexual immorality and infant mortality (to name just a few) were

17 The barefoot tribe of 17 Court, Hospital Street in 1908. The street was aptly named, having one of the highest levels of infant mortality in the city. In the last year of the 19th century 3,400 children died in Birmingham before their first birthday. Overall, there were 74 deaths in Hospital Street in that year, compared to 13 in Inge Street.

all seen as by-products of the drift to the city, and they struck at the heart of the family, the core of society. Many contemporary social commentators, such as Peter Gaskell and Friedrich Engels, saw the advent of 'industrial living' as fracturing the nuclear family. Gaskell writes in 1836:

> A household thus constituted, in which all the decencies and moral observances of domestic life are constantly violated, reduces the inmates to a condition little elevated above that of the savage. Recklessness, improvidence, and unnecessary poverty, starvation, drunkenness, parental cruelty and carelessness, filial disobedience, neglect of conjugal rights, absence of maternal love, destruction of brotherly and sisterly affection, are too often its constituents, and the results of such a combination are moral degradation, ruin of domestic enjoyments, and social misery.

Factory work, which was also mainly an urban phenomenon, was also seen to be affecting the health of the nation, and again there was circumstantial evidence to prove it. There were, of course, no random health checks on industrial workers, but if the men volunteered for the army or applied to the police force they were subject to a complete medical examination. A recruiting sergeant told the Children's Employment Commission in 1843 that, of 613 men examined in Birmingham, only 238 were approved for service.

> The mechanics are shorter, more puny, and altogether inferior in their physical powers; many of the men are distorted in the spine and chest … The mechanics are generally shorter than in any other town I have known, the general height being from five feet four inches to five feet five inches.

The most common reason for rejection was 'want of stamina' (19 men), followed by 'malformation of chest' (nine men) and 'imperfect sight' (six men).

Nor had the catalogue of side-effects finished here. Even mental illness was perceived to be growing in the wake of what was called 'mechanical civilisation'. It must have been growing—there were statistics to prove it. In 1807 a total of 2.26 persons per 100,000 had been defined as insane; by 1890 the figure had risen to 29.6 per 100,000.

But it was not simply the numbers that turned those in power against the city; there was qualitative data too. From the 1840s onwards writers of reports and newspaper articles, novels and pamphlets, queued up to condemn the state of the Victorian city. Edwin Chadwick lamented its lack of sanitation; Henry Mayhew charted the lives of those who clung to its edges; Charles Dickens cried out against the degradation of its poverty.

Those who knew only too well what the inner city meant in terms of life and death, good and evil, were the urban missionaries, sent out by their chapels (as if they were heading for darkest Africa) under the twin banners of charity and evangelism. John Palfrey, describing a day in his missionary work in Birmingham in the 1860s, writes:

> I preceded to an old shop over a brewhouse; when I entered, the first thing I saw was a dead child in the left hand corner of the room, on the right hand the father lying in great agony, and the mother was in a destitute state. By the fire-place sat a man on an old stool; I spoke to him about his soul ...

The missionary employed by the Unitarian mission in Hurst Street in 1892 had somewhat more practical assistance to lend, though the outward circumstances were little altered:

> Household consisting of husband, wife, and four children. Husband has been out of work for months; wife lying on bare mattress in one corner of the room; dead child in another. No fire or food in the house, and scarcely an article of furniture. Assisted with blankets, medical attendance, nourishment, food etc.

Death in the poor family was not only an emotional trauma, it was a financial disaster too. The Funeral Reform Association estimated the cost of 'a handsome funeral' for a working man in 1881 at a little under £12, a sum that could only be met by membership of a burial club. Without such provision the cost of a simple burial could be crippling, even if the family dispensed with the extras: the gloves, the tip for the coachman and the traditional beef, pickles and beer for neighbours and friends. However, the campaign to limit the expectations and to reduce the cost of funerals was still many years ahead in the 1840s. More pressing at the outset was a means of reducing the numbers of those needing one.

It was recognised early, by men like Dr Farr and any missionary entering the homes of the urban poor, that the figures for average life expectancy were seriously distorted by the high rate of childhood mortality. Every year in Victorian England 100,000 children died before their first birthday, a figure that hardly fell throughout the 64 long years of Victoria's reign. Nor did this figure include what Farr estimated to be the 40,000 still-births each year which were not reported to, or recorded by, the local registrar. In some districts of Birmingham, Liverpool and Manchester almost half the infants died before the age of five. Once that critical barrier had been passed, life expectancy rose appreciably.

The death-traps lying in wait for the young child were legion. There were the killer infections such as diphtheria, whooping-cough (often called chin-cough)

18 This has become the classic image of the Birmingham back-to-backs, with all the essential ingredients of poverty, dirt and darkness. It shows three-storey back-to-backs at the rear of 12-13 Upper Priory and dates from c.1872. In such surroundings it was no wonder that the back-to-backers of Leeds were described as 'living at the bottom of wells'.

and especially diarrhoea. These were, in many ways, the more mundane of the killers. Epidemics of measles, smallpox and typhoid also attacked at regular intervals. In 1897, for example, measles claimed the lives of 414 in Birmingham alone, all of the victims being under ten years of age. In his annual report for this year the Medical Officer of Health commented:

> This is certainly the most astounding sacrifice of young lives, especially from an complaint which, if properly looked after, is by no means very [sic] fatal. It is, I think, a serious reflection upon the hygienic education of the community that such a death-toll should be possible.

Added to that there were the side-effects of domestic life, ones that warranted the attention of the local coroner. The over-laying of children, suffocated in a bed they shared with adults, was a common occurrence. So too was getting too close to an open fire, or to a boiling pan of water. And at the opposite end of the temperature scale the lack of warmth in a family that skimped on fuel took its toll as well. As late as 1893 Birmingham's MOH noted that the cold (along with the chest infections that frequently followed) was 'a prolific cause of infant mortality'.

We now know what were the two major factors behind this high death-toll. First there was the endemic overcrowding of the inner city, a situation to which the back-to-backs had contributed hugely. It was not simply the close proximity of the houses to each other, it was the overcrowding within the houses themselves, where families of ten or more people shared two, or at most, three rooms. In such a confined environment epidemics such as measles and influenza spread rapidly and thoroughly. Ironically medical opinion has today turned away from this. Recent research suggests that children are less likely to be affected by asthma if the houses they live in are not spotlessly clean and are shared with brothers, sisters and pets. Our rising standard of living has replaced epidemic with allergy.

Even more fatal was the close proximity of water supply and human waste. Georgian and early Victorian towns lacked either a water pipe or a sewage disposal pipe. Where water was supplied to the court it usually came via a stand-pipe or pump connected to an underground well. Human waste, deposited in an earth-closet, remained where it fell until disposal officers, known euphemistically as nightsoil men, came to collect it. By then the damage had often been done: excrement and waste had flooded out and polluted the water supply. This was the way that cholera and typhoid infiltrated their way so effortlessly through Victorian England.

Such are the advantages of hindsight. The first Victorians were not blessed with such knowledge. It was not until 1849 that Dr William Budd and Dr John Snow identified that cholera was 'a living organism ... which was taken by the act of swallowing it, which multiplied in the intestine by self-propagation'. By then two major epidemics of Asiatic cholera had swept through the country. The first came in 1831-2, when around 32,000 people died; the second arrived in 1848-9, when the death-toll was double this figure.

One example may serve to show how difficult it was to fight a disease whose cause was as yet unknown. In 1849 the Asiatic cholera was sweeping through the Black Country. Willenhall's Committee of Health, therefore, voted to buy more paint brushes. This may seem an unusual moment to repaint the town, but paint brushes were one

of the ways that Victorian society combated this mysterious and deadly disease. Out they went into the slums and back-to-backs and lime-washed the walls, disinfecting them to a height of four or five feet and hoping that this kept at bay the filth and contamination that was thought to be one of the causes of the outbreak.

This was not the first time that cholera had visited the Black Country. In 1832 an outbreak that had centred on Wolverhampton and Bilston had devastated those communities, causing 2,300 deaths and affecting a quarter of the latter's population. On that occasion the local vicar had blamed the outbreak on the immoderate and licentious celebration of the Bilston wake, which had brought God's punishment down upon the whole community. Seventeen years later the authorities were not quite as naive and unprepared, though they were still hampered by an ignorance as to how exactly the disease spread. By a combination of folklore, instinct and imperfect knowledge they prepared as best they could. The first death was reported on 17 August.

Defence was a mixture of prevention and cure. Perhaps the most successful was to put deodorising powder down the drains, together with 'Dr Maccann's mixture', one of many such potions on the market. Another precaution was to burn the bed (usually a flock bed) and bed clothes of any victim, supplying a replacement bed for the victim's family. However, it was noted in the committee minutes that one or two unscrupulous individuals were setting fire to their beds simply in order to get a new one, courtesy of the Health Committee. There are people on the make even in times of distress.

19 Thomas Street in 1875. Much of the street was bull-dozed as part of Joseph Chamberlain's Improvement Scheme shortly after this photograph was taken. The committee's chairman said of Thomas Street in this year: 'Little else is to be seen but bowing roofs, tottering chimneys, tumble down and disused shopping, heaps of bricks, broken windows, and coarse, rough pavements, damp and soggy.'

In addition, bread and meat were distributed to needy families and brandy was also administered to sufferers. It is unlikely that this had any effect, but it was probably better than lying there miserably without any.

Finally—and this was undoubtedly the most expensive protection of all—the bodies of victims were removed and buried as quickly as was humanly and humanely possible. The committee purchased an extra supply of coffins and hired additional hearses and horses from Cannock. Even then, with around 25 burials a day by the end of August, the local coffin-maker was struggling to meet the increase in trade. What's more, the local churchyard too was feeling the strain and a new burial ground was needed. And so the land set aside for a new National School was diverted to a far grimmer function: Willenhall's first purpose-built plague pit.

All this was done, it has to be said, without any help or advice from the government's newly-established General Board of Health. Word had come from London on 3 September 1849 that the Board were too busy to send a representative to the Midlands. By the time an officer was despatched in mid-September the cholera tide was ebbing. He congratulated the local board on its efforts and left. It is believed that well over 300 people had died from the disease in the seven weeks during which it had raged. At the end of the following year the Willenhall Board proposed a vote of thanks 'to Almighty God for that gracious providence by which, in the midst of serious sickness and mortality, their lives had been spared.' Clearly Willenhall had more support in heaven than Bilston.

Thus the Victorian towns muddled along, without any clear sense of what they were doing. What is remarkable, in the absence of hard scientific evidence, is that their instincts were often right, even if the reasoning behind them was not. Cesspools and open sewers were indeed a health hazard, though not in exactly the way they were perceived. For that first generation of Victorians it was the pythogenic theory of disease which held sway, a belief that decaying matter gave off a miasma or effluvium which infected those within range of it. This idea, not truly challenged until the 1870s, lay behind Edwin Chadwick's pioneering *Report on the Sanitary Conditions of the Labouring Classes*, published in 1842 under the auspices of the Poor Law Board, of which Chadwick was secretary. This report, ably assisted by the 1848/9 cholera epidemic, turned heads, but there were others harping on the same theme. William Farr wrote thus of London's 'Great Stink':

> The exhalation from sewers, churchyards, vaults, slaughter-houses,
> cesspools commingles in the atmosphere ... and nothwithstanding
> the wonderful provision of nature for the speedy oxidation of organic
> matter in water and air, accumulates, and the density of the poison ... is
> sufficient to impress its destructive action on the living ... to connect by

a subtle, sickly, deadly medium, the people agglomerated in narrow
streets and courts, down which the wind does not blow, and upon which
the sun seldom shines.

Equally, those who were visiting schools for the Birmingham Statistical
Society for the Improvement of Education in 1838 turned up their noses at 'the
effluvia arising from the dress of the scholars mingled with the close air'.

Was it any wonder, then, that a strange tug-of-war broke out in the enclosed
courts, with health officers pushing windows open to encourage the circulation
of air, and occupants pulling them shut to keep in the warmth? As Councillor
Middlemore rather wittily told the Artisans' Dwellings Enquiry in Birmingham
in 1884:

> I have seen the sky though the ceiling and walls of many bedrooms,
> and it is clear that this is not the tenant's fault, for I am afraid that he
> dislikes the fresh air which these holes admit.

Like the mythical miasma itself, the theory of it percolated through the
community. When Robert Rawlinson presented his report on the sanitary
condition of the borough of Birmingham to the General Board of Health in 1849
it included the following memorandum from the aggrieved residents of George
Road in Edgbaston:

> … they frequently experience great annoyance from the highly
> disagreeable effluvia which proceeds from the drains in their
> neighbourhood; that the noxious character of these effluvia is but
> too apparent from the suffering health and frequent fevers that have
> prevailed in many of the houses …

'Drains?' a hard-pressed inhabitant of central Birmingham might have exclaimed.
'They have drains and they still complain?'

But whatever mistaken beliefs Edwin Chadwick and Robert Rawlinson
may have perpetuated about miasmata, what was highly significant about their
reports was the connection they made between poor housing and poor health.
Chadwick opens his narration on this very theme:

> In the manufacturing towns of England, most of which have enlarged
> with great rapidity, the additions have been made without regard to
> either the personal comfort of the inhabitants or the necessities which
> congregation requires. To build the largest number of cottages on the
> smallest allowable space seems to have been the original view of the
> speculators, and the having the houses up and tenanted, the *ne plus*

ultra of their desires. Thus neighbourhoods have arisen in which there
is neither water nor out-offices, nor any convenience for the absolute
domestic wants of the occupiers.

Simply put, in cutting down on space and sanitation, the builders and landowners
were cutting short the lives of their tenants. As Moore Bayley told an enquiry on
working-class housing in Birmingham as late as 1901:

> I could show you a list of names of 'swells' at Edgbaston, living in their
> big houses, who own property in Birmingham which is a disgrace to the
> landlords, who are guilty of moral murder … Here are poor people unable
> to secure proper accommodation and with the accommodation they have
> to put up with, typhus, typhoid and premature death are thrown in for
> the rent.

There were many other good examples to prove Chadwick's point, and Leeds
was as bad as any. The Royal Commission on the Health of Towns, to which we
have already referred, had the following to say of the town in 1845:

> But by far the most unhealthy localities of Leeds are close squares of
> houses, or yards, as they are called, which have been erected for the
> accommodation of working people. Some of these, though situated
> on comparatively high ground, are airless from the enclosed structure,
> and, being wholly unprovided with any form of under-drainage, or
> convenience, or arrangements for cleaning, are one mass of damp and
> filth. In some instances I found cellars, or under-rooms, with from
> two to six inches of water standing over the floors, and putrid from its
> stagnation in one case, from receiving the soakage of slopwater standing
> in pools in the street adjoining. The ashes, garbage and filth of all kinds
> are thrown from the doors and windows of the houses upon the surface
> of the streets and courts …

Many other instances in the report dwelt more on the unpleasant, sanitary
aspects of the situation, but the main point was clear enough. Whatever rose-
tinted respect many Victorians had for the Middle Ages, reproducing the state
of its towns was not an ideal starting-point for a Gothic Revival. As one of the
contributors to *Punch* rhymed in 1874:

> The cottage-homes of England—
> Alas, how strong they smell!
> There's fever in the cesspool,
> And sewage in the well.

From the publication of Edwin Chadwick's report onwards, battle was joined. On the one side there was light, space and ventilation, on the other damp, darkness and disease. But if that was the simple state of affairs, the solution might have been quickly found. In reality this was a far deeper conflict, and one that went to the heart of Victorian Britain, to the questions of land ownership, private property and the role of the state.

'The poorest man may in his cottage bid defiance to all the forces of the Crown!' William Pitt had once thundered from the despatch box. 'It may be frail—the roof may shake—the wind may blow through it—the storm may enter—the rain may enter—but the King of England may not enter …' Pitt's rallying cry for the Englishman's castle, enshrined (it has to be said) more in belief than in law, seems strangely prophetic, given the state of urban housing by the middle of the 19th century. It was, of course, at odds with the reality of home-ownership, where few Englishmen actually owned their own house, but such sentiments were common enough. English resistance to government interference—what is dismissively referred to as 'the nanny state'—is deep-seated, and it applies equally to how fast we drive our cars, where we park them, whether we have identity cards, or how straight we want our bananas. It is, as the man or woman in the street will often say, a free country, and the ethos of individualism is near the heart of our sense of national and personal identity. It is not, we might add, at the heart of Europe, where owner-occupiers are fewer and state intervention greater.

Such independence of spirit could be and was applied to the issue of housing. A handful of towns in the 1840s—Liverpool, Bristol, and Blackburn among them—applied for local Acts to control their new housing, whether applied to the space a building occupied or to the materials with which it was constructed. But the attempt to dictate standards nationally met overwhelming resistance, both at select committee stage and when Lord Normanby's Building Regulations Bill reached the Commons in 1842. Endless petitions from builders and landowners, as well as from local authorities, declared such legislation 'highly injurious to rights and property', and the Bill fell in consequence. Such attitudes died hard. As late as 1875, when Birmingham Corporation proposed weekly sanitary inspections of the worst courts in the borough, it met with tough resistance in the Council chamber. Alderman Osborne declared the proposals 'unconstitutional and un-English' and added that:

> … they would, if carried out in their integrity, prove most vexatious, offensive, and oppressive to the inhabitants of the borough, by subjecting them to the constant domiciliary visits of the inspectors, thus violating that which has been hitherto held most dear to Englishmen—namely, the sanctity of domestic life.

The inviolability of private property was a banner behind which many would energetically march, and those most affected by decaying and insanitary homes did not have the vote to swing opinion in any other direction. This was, after all, the age of self-help and *laissez-faire*, and it applied as much to house-owning as it did to the economy.

Edwin Chadwick railed against what he saw as 'petty and sinister interests' at work in local government, but Chadwick probably overestimated the popularity of his campaign among the general public. Cheap, shoddy and unwatered houses were there not only because builders put them up, but also because they were the best that their inhabitants could afford. The 1886 Royal Commission on the Housing of the Working Classes estimated that 85 per cent of families paid one-fifth of their income in rent, and almost 50 per cent paid as much as a quarter or a half. Landlords who made improvements to their properties, or built them to a higher specification, inevitably passed on the costs in increased rents, and the transformation of a two-shilling house into a three-shilling one was often enough to tip a family into poverty and hardship or (more likely) to send them packing. The town clerk of Leeds told the Royal Commission on Health of Towns in 1841 that banning back-to-backs would only drive people into the even less salubrious lodging-houses, because they could not, or would not, pay higher rents.

Even this assumed that the property owner could afford to make improvements in the first place. As one builder, Thomas Cubitt, touchingly told the same committee in 1840, the average owner was 'a little shopkeeper class of person, who has saved a little money in business ...' There could hardly have been a dry eye in the committee room after that. There was equal reluctance to introduce piped water or mains drainage into courts, even where such provision was possible. The charge made by water company or local authority was again likely to hit the pocket of the house-holder. And so the back-to-back courts continued to be built. As late as 1884 the Leeds MOH was confessing to the Royal Commission on Housing that 'the working people of Leeds would rather have back-to-backs than houses open at the back ...' It was not simply the difference between warmth and draught, or between tradition and innovation, it was the difference between 3s. and 6s. a week.

But like it or not, national legislation did in the end arrive. Indeed, there was hardly an area of Victorian life in which there was more legislation than in public health and housing. But the delicate balancing act between concern and compulsion remained for much of the century. The Public Health Act of 1848, for example, set out national standards for local authorities, but they were not mandatory. The appointment of a medical officer and a system of inspection remained optional. So too the Local Government Act of 1858 and the Public Health Act of 1875. Here were offered model bye-laws, outlining minimum size

of rooms and windows, width of streets, standards of drainage and sanitation and so on, but again it was left to local councils to decide whether to adopt, amend or ignore them.

It was a slow process, but the slow drip, drip, drip of legislation was preferable to that from a leaking roof. By 1882 around 1,600 local authorities, both urban and rural, possessed a set of housing bye-laws modelled on those recommended in the Acts. Though not yet officially outlawed, the back-to-back court was becoming a thing of the past. It was, I suppose, an unfortunate irony that the drive towards uniformity of legislation resulted in a dull uniformity of housing. The endless ribbons of identical terraced houses in identical streets which still ring our towns today were not to everyone's taste, but they were undoubtedly an improvement on what had gone before.

The Acts already referred to, and the bye-laws attached to them, dealt with standards for new building, and improvements to those already in existence, but

20 Gardens in Bournville in the 1940s. While civic authorities wrestled with the problem of the central wards in the 1870s, George Cadbury voted with his feet and moved his chocolate works out to Bournbrook, three miles from the city centre. Here he created the first 'garden suburb', with a view to engendering both a sense of community and a healthier lifestyle among his workers.

where did this leave houses no longer considered fit for habitation? Given that many of the courts of the inner cities had been built in the early years of the 19th century, this was becoming an increasing issue by the 1870s. There were two more pieces of legislation to deal with this. In 1868 was passed the Artisans' and Labourers' Dwellings Act, generally referred to as the Torrens Act after the backbencher who introduced it. Under the terms of this Act local authorities had the power to close any house considered unfit by a medical officer of health, and to demand improvement or demolition by its owner. Despite its humble, backbench origins, the Torrens Act remained the model for local action well into the 1960s.

More wide-reaching were the powers of the Artisans' and Labourers' Dwellings Improvement Act of 1875, sometimes called the Cross Act after the Home Secretary in Disraeli's government. The Cross Act established the right to

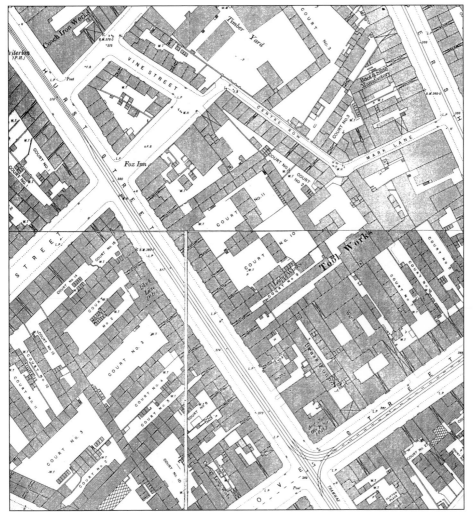

21 The Hurst Street area on the 1:500 Ordnance Survey map, surveyed in 1887. The map gives a good idea of the varying size of back-to-back courts, squeezed into every available plot. Court 15 can be seen opposite the *Fox Inn*. Excavations in the yard of Court 15 during renovation confirmed the position of the water-tap on the far wall of the court. The map shows that a number of courts were still relying on wells.

demolish a whole area, if the houses were considered unfit for human habitation, or if poor housing was the cause of poor health. Here lay the origins of the huge slum clearance schemes and the compulsory purchase orders that swept through the nation in the 20th century. Initially, however, take-up was slow and only 32 such schemes had been completed by the First World War. It was not difficult to see the reason for this. Unlike the Torrens Act, implementation of the 1875 Act cost money; local authorities had to buy the land and property (at market price) and to pay for demolition. In addition, the Cross Act stipulated that an improvement scheme should 'provide for the accommodation of at least as many members of the working class as may be displaced ...' The way local councils delayed and ducked such responsibility is an object lesson in the relationship between local and national government, and the offending clause was removed in 1882.

22 Joseph Chamberlain (1836-1914). During his three years as Mayor of Birmingham Chamberlain energetically pursued what was called 'gas and water socialism'—the municipal takeover of utilities. And the profits from the gas undertaking were in turn ploughed into the Improvement Scheme, which transformed 93 acres of the town centre.

It was, therefore, only the most ambitious and confident of corporations that sent in the bulldozers under the Cross Act, and one such was Birmingham. Under the leadership of Joseph Chamberlain and wedded to the message of the Civic Gospel, Birmingham was beginning to flex its political muscles by the 1870s. In 1874 alone the Corporation municipalised the gas industry by buying the two companies which supplied it, and effected a hostile take-over of the Birmingham Waterworks Co. too. In the following year Chamberlain launched his Improvement Scheme to clear 93 acres of the town centre, and to rebuild the area for commercial use.

The Birmingham Improvement Scheme cost around £1.75 million, somewhat offset by profits from the gas industry and the sale of leases on Corporation Street. The latter was planned to be almost a mile long, but the economic slump of the early 1880s prevented its completion. The whole scheme owed much, if not all, to Joseph Chamberlain's municipal vision and financial adroitness. It was audacious and long-sighted, but it was hardly in the spirit of the Cross Act. True, a number of unsavoury streets—the Minories, Oxygen Street and Lower Priory among them—were removed, but so were cherry orchards and the grand

(if decaying) houses of Old Square. Chamberlain had in truth engineered a redevelopment scheme under the umbrella of the Cross Act.

As for those displaced by the scheme, there was to be no alternative accommodation. The new town centre contained law courts and offices, shops and winter gardens, but it most assuredly did not include working-class housing. As Alderman Cook told a local enquiry on the workings of the Act in 1884: 'when it was accepted no one dreamed that we were going to destroy 855 dwellings without putting any artisans' houses in their place.' *The Dart*, a Liberal weekly not in the Chamberlain camp, had a more witty way of putting it:

> New Birmingham recipe for lowering the death-rate of an insanitary
> area. Pull down nearly all the houses and make the inhabitants move
> somewhere else.
> 'Tis an excellent plan and I'll tell you for why.
> Where there's no person living no person can die.

Only in 1889, and with some reluctance, did the Corporation erect 102 artisans'

23 The Birmingham Court and Alley Concerts Association was founded in 1898, following a similar move in Liverpool, to give free musical performances for those who were unlikely to have the price of a ticket for the Town Hall. As many as 4,000 people attended some concerts. Here the band strikes up in Tower Street during the 1908 season.

24 Children enjoying a court concert in 1907. The association's annual report says of one concert attended by the Lord Mayor: 'We believe that his lordship was deeply impressed by what he saw and heard—particularly by the preparations made for the reception of the concert party in the way of decorating, and the thorough cleansing and swilling of the large court from top to bottom, the attention with which the music was listened to and the evident delight it yielded ...'.

cottages on the far northern edge of the area in Lawrence Street and Ryder Street, on land that had attracted no commercial interest. But such dwellings, let at between 5s 6d and 7s a week, were well beyond the pocket of most of those who had formerly lived in the area. In 1884 there were still some 27,000 families in Birmingham paying rent of less than 3s 6d.

The experience of Birmingham here is worth noting. Here was a local authority at the height of its powers, with a supreme confidence in its mission to improve and elevate the lives of its citizens, and where libraries, baths, parks and schools came as standard. Yet it (and many others) were highly reluctant to usurp the rights of the private enterprise when it came to building homes. And even if Birmingham and others had been willing to cross that sacred line, there were still serious doubts whether local government could provide houses cheap enough for that impoverished lower tier. 'A local authority can build at less cost than any in the private sector', Alderman Cook had also told the enquiry, 'and yet it cannot provide houses at less than 4s a week.' The age of the council house was still some way into the future.

FOUR

Running to Stand Still

The relentless pace of industrialisation and urbanisation in the 18th and 19th centuries had left in its wake considerable problems in the housing stock of this country. These problems (in the eyes of the legislators, at least) were seen principally in terms of sanitation and health, not in the nature of the houses themselves. The culmination of that campaign was the national ban on new back-to-backs in 1909, and came in the wake of a report commissioned by the Local Government Board. Dr L. W. Darra Mair had been directed by the Board to study the comparative death-rates in back-to-backs and throughs (the contemporary term for a house with a front and back door) in the West Riding of Yorkshire. Dr Mair's findings served to confirm the disadvantages of the former, even when they were recently constructed and fitted with water-closets. On average, mortality was higher by 15 to 20 per cent in the back-to-backs. Mair concluded:

> The outstanding causes of death which produced the excess of mortality in back-to-back houses were: pneumonia, bronchitis and other pulmonary diseases ... and diseases of defective development and of malnutrition in young children. The corrected excess of mortality from each of these two groups of diseases in back-to-back houses approached 40 per cent.

That is, a child was almost twice as likely to die if he or she was raised in a back-to-back than in a terraced house.

By this date, the attention of authorities and campaigners had moved away from simply matters of health to the nature of the houses themselves. The shift in attitude, therefore, towards bad housing in itself that appears towards the end of the Victorian era is a significant one. But first let us remind ourselves of the nature of much of the house building in the 19th century. An article in *Public Health* for 1901, if rather sweeping, summarises the position pretty well:

> The evolution of the jerry-built houses appears to be somewhat as follows: some green fields, or some mansion with a few acres of pleasure or garden ground, conveniently situated in the suburbs, are advertised to be sold, or let on building leases. Timber is forthwith cut down, roads formed, and sewers built; plans are prepared by which the ground is cut up into plots containing a few feet of frontage and a great number of

RUNNING TO STAND STILL / 47

feet for depth. These plots, if not sold, are let at ground rent at so many pounds each, the lessee undertaking to put a house of specified value upon it. By these means it is intended that a field, which at the time of letting brings in a few shillings per annum as grazing ground, shall, when covered with houses, bring in as many pounds, and that, moreover, the houses erected thereon shall revert to the ground landlord at the termination of the lease. But to get the house built something more is needed. The capitalist, often the owner of the land, now comes forward with loans, to enable a class of small builders to undertake the work. These builders, for the most part men with little or no means, but with a certain knowledge and experience, have to build the houses and support themselves and their families during the period in which the loans can be made to last. A surveyor is appointed to protect the advances of loans, and if he proves faithful to his employer, the brick, lime and timber merchants, and others, will probably suffer by the bankruptcy of the builder. But if the builder is not to fail, it follows that he must go to the cheapest market for the materials. His bricks will be porous, his timber shaky, his mortar deficient in lime, his plaster destitute of hair, his woodwork and joinery of the most unsatisfactory kind, and his sanitary appliances of the cheapest quality.

There were plenty of examples to prove the point. A carpenter giving evidence to the 1884 housing enquiry in Birmingham gave detailed descriptions of deal being used instead of elm in closet seats, and of doors only an inch and a quarter thick. 'Some of the doors were so thin,' he commented, 'that they were liable to be broken by slamming ...'

The building bye-laws of the 1860s and 1870s—driven by Victorian obsessions with space, ventilation and materials—had been intended to address these issues, but the new regulations not only raised the cost of building, they also affected the density of housing. W. S. Till, the Birmingham borough surveyor, told the same enquiry that it was now only permitted to build nine houses where 18 or 20 had been possible before, whilst an estate agent added that the cost of building had risen by a third since the bye-laws had been introduced. The result, simply put, was that in swerving to avoid a crisis of health and sanitation, Britain had driven straight into a housing emergency instead. And with the continuing rise in the population—health improved, mortality lowered—it was an emergency that was becoming more acute by the day.

There was a mounting housing shortage before the First World War, not made easier by the lack of building during the war. By 1918 the national shortage had risen to some 600,000, and any plan to demolish sub-standard accommodation had to take this into account. In Birmingham—not the worst case by any means—43,366 back-to-backs still housed 200,000 people. There was no separate water supply for 42,020 houses and 52,028 had no separate lavatory. But as the annual report of the Ministry of Health put it in 1921: 'until much more has been done to overcome the existing shortage of housing accommodation, it would be extremely unwise to attempt to put into operation drastic measures for clearing unhealthy areas.'

Yet change was on its way, surfing a wave of self-sacrifice and expectation raised up by war. David Lloyd George's slogan for the General Election campaign of 1918—'homes fit for heroes'—set the tone for the post-war years. Christopher Addison's Housing & Town Planning Act of 1919 made it obligatory for local authorities to assess and address the housing needs of their citizens. From this point forward councils, supported by government subsidies, were to be the chief agents in housing provision, although the Act gave subsidies both to local authorities and to private builders. Under its terms 213,000 houses were built, though these were expensive: the government was paying £800 for houses that cost only £300 to build. Not surprisingly then, the funds fell victim to the recession of 1921-2.

Each new government from the 1920s to 1950s inherited some sort of housing crisis from its predecessor, but the solutions (usually cut short by problems in the economy) inevitably reflected the political slant of the administration. In 1923, for example, the new Conservative government passed another Act—Neville Chamberlain's Housing Act of 1923—giving new subsidies to private builders. Under this measure a further 438,000 houses were built, until the Act was withdrawn in 1929.

Under the first (short-lived) Labour government, Wheatley's Housing Act of 1924 increased the subsidy to local authorities for building at controlled rents. This progressive measure led to the building of another 520,000 houses, until this Act in turn was terminated in 1932.

During the 1930s cheaper materials—especially in the Midlands, London and the south-east—contributed to a housing boom. Birmingham Corporation alone built 51,681 houses in the decade, enough to accommodate 200,000 people, while the private sector built a further 59,744 houses. In such provision Birmingham exceeded all other authorities, having completed 30,000 council houses by 1930 and 40,000 by 1933. It was estimated that by 1939 about a third of Birmingham's one million inhabitants lived in houses built since the Great War. As a result only 18.8 per cent of the city's working classes still lived in the central slum area, compared with 27.6 per cent in 1921.

Overall, local authorities built a total of 1.1 million houses between the wars, while private builders put up a further 400,000 with government subsidies

25 *(opposite)* Court in Rupert Street, Nechells, in 1908. Despite being outside the city centre, Nechells had a high proportion of houses rented at 3s 6d or less a week, and infant mortality was 50 per cent above the city average. In 1947 the suburbs of Duddeston and Nechells were designated as one of Birmingham's five 'Central Redevelopment Areas' and were the first to be demolished.

26 3 Court, Bagot Street, in 1904. One solution to the perennial problem of poor ventilation and overcrowding was to convert a pair of back-to-backs into a single 'through' house. This was done in some cases, but was only possible when the houses had been built sufficiently well to withstand conversion. And, of course, the landlord expected to double the rent. Such a converted house might rent for 14s in the 1930s.

and 2.5 million without. In all then, a staggering four million houses had been erected. It was perhaps where government social policy between the wars was most successful.

Yet in spite of all this effort, the slums remained, and they remained because slum clearance had never really been government policy, only a useful spin-off from it. It had been hoped that the mass house-building programmes would squeeze out the slums by a process known as 'filtering up'. As new homes became available, so (in theory) the old homes would steadily empty. In reality, however, most of these new homes were snapped up by the better off, leaving those at the bottom of the property ladder still stuck in their old courts. It was Arthur Greenwood's 1930 Housing Act that changed all that. Here for the first time 'unfitness for human habitation' was defined in law, and the machinery for compulsory purchase and slum clearance was streamlined. It has altered little in the 70-odd years since. Under the Greenwood umbrella local councils were given funding for demolition, and in return were obliged to draw up five-year plans for slum clearance. The terms of the subsidy also show a major change of emphasis. Each authority was to receive a subsidy of £2 5s for 40 years for every person re-housed, enough of an inducement to send council officials to their maps in droves. By the outbreak of the Second World War unfit houses were being removed at a rate of 90,000 a year.

It might be useful at this point to outline briefly what had become of the nation's housing stock, or at least the houses that accommodated the majority of the population. There was still a core of back-to-backs and blind-backs, increasingly confined to the inner ring of many cities. Most of these were now provided with piped water, but still shared WCs and wash-houses with the rest of the court. Next up on the social scale were the long rows of tunnel-backs of the middle ring, raised up in their thousands by speculative builders working under the Victorian bye-law standards. The name derived from the tunnels or passages (or gunnels or gulleys) that ran in between the rows. Such houses had a 'best' or parlour room at the front, with a living room and kitchen, scullery and toilet behind, though the latter was usually detached from the house. Upstairs were two larger bedrooms and a third smaller one over the scullery. In the Victorian period, when the tunnel-back was the aspiration of the clerk and higher earning artisan, this room would have been occupied by the all-purpose general servant, who came as part of the aspirational package. By the First World War, however, the supply of servants had dried up and the room had become another family bedroom.

But not all tunnel-backs were the same. There were further distinctions to sub-divide the classes. At one end were the houses entered directly from the street, where the sanctity of the front parlour was never quite as pure. At the other end was the tunnel-back with a front garden, though the garden was less important in itself than for the space it allowed for a bay window, that essential icon of respectability. Here the entrance was into a hall which, for all its darkness, helped to preserve the individual character of the other rooms, and as a result the parlour could be set aside for Sunday visitors alone.

Finally, and decidedly into the realm of the middle classes, lay what was called 'the universal plan' house. This had emerged in the course of the vast building programmes of the period after the Great War, and followed meekly in the footsteps of the Garden City developments of the late 19th century. House designs of this type show a return to traditional and vernacular design, spacious, light and well-ventilated. We could call them 20th-century cottages, brick-built and with pitched roofs. But their appeal was not unanimous. Just as the Victorian court dwellers had resisted the drive towards ventilation, so the new architectural model was not to the liking of the Women's Co-operative Guild, who argued for separate parlours, rather than through-plan living rooms.

Such houses, built in pairs or blocks of four or six, were wider than the widest tunnel-backs, with a hall that led directly into the scullery/kitchen, thus preserving the privacy of both parlour and living room. Upstairs were three bedrooms, plus a bathroom and probably a linen cupboard. With a frontage of around 20 feet wide and the obligatory bay window, the 'universal' house presented a more confident face to the world than the 13-foot terrace. Such homes must have seemed the lap of luxury for those moving out. They had their own water supply, as well as hot water, either from a kitchen boiler or one behind the living-room fire. But as the estates grew so the overall quality often deteriorated, leaving monotony and poor construction. These houses were being erected both as council houses and for private ownership. Renting a suburban house cost around 10s a week by the late 1930s, but by this date the possibility of owner-occupation was coming within the budget of an increasing number of families. The average wage stood at around £3 15s a week, enough to meet a mortgage repayment of perhaps £1 a week. This would buy a standard three-bedroom house at a cost of some £600.

It's evident from this period of universal housing that there was a new spirit of optimism and a conscious rejection of the past in this period, one that we associate more with the post-war era. Housing was shifting, geographically outwards and away from the two-up, one-down of the courts. The slums of the central areas were visibly shrinking, to be replaced by mostly suburban estates. In Birmingham such estates often hugged the city's outer edges. Kingstanding (begun in 1930 with the purchase of Kettlehouse Farm) was the largest council estate in Europe, with 4,802 houses. But even this was only slightly bigger than others at Fox Hollies, Lea Hall, Billesley and Weoley Castle. These new estates swallowed up huge amounts of land, with densities of no more than 12 houses to the acre. Such was the density recommended in the Tudor Walters report on the standards of local authority housing in 1919, and it was in marked contrast to the 60 houses per acre of the courts. Out in the rural hinterland space could be lavishly distributed; while the bye-law builders had been niggardly with streets, the new generation of planners wove geometrical patterns of cul-de-sacs and crescents. But such generosity of spirit came at a price: the need for more land led to the annexation of the neighbouring villages of Perry Barr (1927), and Castle Bromwich and Sheldon (1931). This was the world encountered with a deep patriotic distaste by J.B. Priestley during his *English Journey* of 1933:

> The third England, I concluded, was the new post-war England, belonging far more to the age itself than to this particular island. America, I suppose, was its real birthplace. This is the England of arterial by-pass roads, of filling stations and factories that look like exhibition buildings, of giant cinemas and dance-halls and cafes, bungalows with tiny garages, cocktail bars, Woolworth's, motor-coaches, wireless, hiking, factory girls looking like actresses, greyhound racing and dirt tracks, swimming pools and everything given away for cigarette coupons.

The great rebuilding had created a new landscape in Britain. The new estates were a watered down version of the garden suburb, sometimes suburban and sometimes satellite towns on green-field sites, such as Welwyn Garden City or Norris Green and Speke near Liverpool, or Wythenshawe south of Manchester, with its 7,000 houses, on land given to the city by one of the foremost writers and housing pioneers of the pre-war period, Sir Ernest Simon. They offered an aspiration and an escape for those still trapped in the 19th century and many, like Falstaff on his death-bed, 'babbled o' green fields'.

But many who effected the great escape did not find it as perfect as the brochures. Some occupants disliked being uprooted from the friends and relatives where they used to live; others objected to the increased rents. Houses ranged from 10s to 12s 6d a week, plus rates, well above previous levels, and rent subsidies were not available until after the Second World War. This may have been intentional. Some authorities wanted only better-off tenants on the new estates. The lack of pubs too was sometimes deliberate, as it was in Liverpool. Lack of shops, however, was usually the result of poorly coordinated planning.

There were other complaints too. In the newly expanded suburbia travelling to work could be expensive and problematic. Tenants complained that the fresh air gave their children bigger and costlier appetites, and that furnishing a larger property also added to the cost. The mass building programme also tended towards uniformity and inflexibility of size. Two-thirds of all inter-war council houses had three bedrooms, only 4.3 per cent had one bedroom and 3.7 per cent had four. A regulation size of family had clearly been built into the planning.

Often house building greatly exceeded the social and educational provision needed to serve the new estate. With 9,000 houses Kingstanding was as big as a town like Shrewsbury. But whereas Shrewsbury had 30 churches and 15 church halls and parish rooms, Kingstanding had one church and one hall.

Suburban sprawl added its own difficulties of space and distance. Many of these might have been avoided by erecting flats, but there was little appetite for such 'modern architecture' seen (and often visited by planners) in central Europe and Scandinavia, where blocks of flats were proliferating. Although there was lively and heated debate over the issue of 'houses or flats', most authorities rejected the latter except in the inner city or limited them to four or five storeys. The giant Quarry Hill scheme in Leeds of the late 1930s, which replaced 2,000 slum houses with 938 flats, was a rare exception.

What is incontrovertible, however, is that improved accommodation was having its effect upon the nation's health. The death-rate fell from an average of 13.9 per thousand before the First World War to 11.9 per thousand before the Second. Infant mortality too fell, from 105 per thousand (in 1910) to 56 per thousand in 1940, and deaths from the old killers—tuberculosis, measles, diarrhoea and bronchitis—fell greatly. But here again there were considerable regional variations. The infant mortality figure for 1935 was 47 per thousand in the south-east, but 63 in Wales, 76 in Northumberland and 77 in Scotland.

By the 1930s there was much enthusiasm for, and faith in, centralised planning, and the wholesale rebuilding of Britain's cities. Many of those plans had to be shelved for financial reasons, but were dusted off once the war ended. Building a new Britain was articulated by government as one of its war aims, and Britain emerged from the Second World War in a collectivist fervour to build a 'New Jerusalem'. Yet within less than 25 years that faith and enthusiasm, and many of the schemes themselves, had collapsed.

Changes were already underway before the war ended. The Barlow Commission of 1937, reporting in 1940, is generally seen as the planners' breakthrough, advising greater government control over industrial and urban growth, especially in the south-east. The Scott Report of 1942 suggested a planning system that covered the countryside as well as the town, preserving the best agricultural land from urban sprawl and creating National Parks. The Blitz too gave powerful impetus to rebuilding Britain.

Coventry is a good example of how these two trends came together. It was one of the first cities to set up an Architects' Department, and an exhibition in May-June 1939 showed plans for a redesigned civic centre. These plans were mobilised within weeks of the November 1940 raids. Six months later plans were displayed for a new city centre, with a ring road, zoned development and pedestrianised shopping precincts. It's a sobering fact that more of Coventry was redeveloped by the city planners than by the *Luftwaffe*. Other cities such as Oxford and Sheffield followed close behind. Planning became the decade's key word. The contrast was starkly drawn between blighted landscape, polluted rivers, outdated factories and the close association of housing and workshops, and a freshly planned landscape of wide highways, with zoned development of industry, shops and housing. Such plans were proudly displayed in hundreds of towns. Wartime propaganda made a planned 'tomorrow' one of its centrepieces, and plans for Birmingham found their way into an edition of the *Tripoli Times*, an unexpected reminder of home for the troops in North Africa.

A Ministry of Town and Country Planning (1943) was followed by Town and Country Planning Acts in 1944 and 1947. The greatest expressions of this new optimism were the New Towns, enshrined in the New Towns Act of 1946, setting up development corporations to plan and create them when they were 'expedient in the national interest', and empowering such corporations 'to do anything necessary or expedient for the purposes of the new town …' Fourteen were designated by 1950, eight in the London ring, together covering a population of one million. Another six had been added by the mid-'60s, to accommodate a total of 1.5 million inhabitants.

In addition to this, there was still the pressing need for new houses. Building from 1935 to 1939 was running at 330,000 houses a year, but this was barely enough to meet demand, especially as the population and marriage rate continued to grow. The population of Great Britain rose from 38 million in 1921 to 48 million in 1966. During the war only 5,000 houses a year had been built, and the backlog due for demolition was increasing. In 1939 there were still 550,000 slum homes awaiting demolition, as well as a further 350,000 'marginal dwellings', and bomb damage added a further 475,000 houses to the list. After the war there was the baby boom, increased divorce and the need to accommodate ex-POWs and foreign servicemen who had decided to stay in Britain. Liverpool is a good example of this expanded demand: the combination of houses lost in the war, slum clearance schemes halted and further houses listed as sub-standard, left the city with a demand for 40,000 new houses.

The result was yet another housing crisis. The 1945 Labour government committed itself to an optimistic programme of 240,000 new houses a year, but the competing financial demands of the export drive, the welfare state and acute shortage of materials made this commitment impossible to meet. Provision of pre-fabs in war-damaged cities helped, but were meant only as a temporary measure. By 1951 Labour had built only 900,000 houses, impressive in itself, but well short of the promises.

In the 1951 General Election campaign the Conservative Party committed itself to a programme of 300,000 houses a year, and this was no doubt one of the reasons for its victory. This total was to be achieved by increased subsidies to local government and increased licences to private builders. Remarkably, they met this target, with 319,000 houses in 1953 and a record 348,000 in 1954. Partly this was achieved by allowing local government to devote half of its allocation to private building. The government indicated that council housing should be used only to deal with specific social problems.

The shift away from council housing had begun, made clear by the 1953 White Paper 'Housing: The Next Step' and the 1954 Housing Repairs and Rents Act, which reduced the subsidies for general needs housing while retaining them for slum clearance. The former were entirely removed in 1957. The shift in the balance between tenant and owner-occupier is clear from the statistics. In 1947 owner-occupiers amounted to 26.0 per cent; by 1985 this had reached 61.9 per cent. The numbers of owner-occupiers was boosted further by Margaret Thatcher's Housing Act of 1980, which gave tenants of three years' standing the right to buy their home at much below the market price. Such schemes had been in operation throughout the 1970s, but not on this scale. Inevitably, then, these sell-offs began to reduce the overall stock of council property. Council tenants rose to a maximum of 32 per cent in 1977 before falling back, while the percentage of private tenants fell from 58.0 per cent in 1947 to 8.3 per cent in 1985.

A total of 2.5 million houses were built during the 1950s, but the government was running to stay still, as family and social patterns mutated. The number of

27 Architect's plan for the proposed redevelopment of Duddeston and Nechells from 1943. The demolition of all the Victorian houses and workshops in this area allowed for a complete re-planning of the area, with separate zones for housing (high-rise and low-rise), factories and parks. The idea worked less well on the ground than it did on the map.

young couples, elderly people and tenants no longer able to find accommodation in the private rented sector was growing. In 1964, the year Labour took power, a record 374,000 houses were completed, but demand continued to outstrip supply, and the overall stock was still aging. In 1951 a third of houses were over 80 years old and a third still had no bathroom. One in five houses had no toilet or piped water, and one in twenty did not have a kitchen sink. The number of unfit dwellings had risen from 472,000 at the outbreak of war to 847,000 in 1954. Eleven years later this figure had hardly dropped at all.

Labour's programme in 1964 was for 500,000 houses a year, equally divided between the public and private sector. Like previous administrations it fell short, despite having produced 1.8 million houses by 1969. An inspection in 1967 showed the housing stock continuing to deteriorate, with 1.8 million houses considered unfit, a further 3.7 million needing repair and 2.3 million lacking indoor sanitation. Wholesale slum clearance schemes did not always help matters, with their tendency to sweep away housing that often needed no more than repair and upgrading. At the same time the rented sector was continuing to reduce, and was getting a very bad press. Notorious instances of Rachmanism led to the fair rents

28 Director, Ken Loach, and writer, Jeremy Sandford, on the 'set' of *Cathy Come Home* in November 1966. The central section of the play was filmed in and around the courts of Hingeston Street in the Winson Green area of Birmingham. Cathy and her partner are evicted for being unable to pay the rent, and cannot find the 'key money' for another house. The play's deceptively realistic style brought much unwelcome publicity to the city's housing department.

29 Back of 103 Hingeston Street, Winson Green, in November 1966. Given the difficulties of drying a large family wash indoors, a windy day was a godsend to the hard-pressed housewife. Everything from a gas lamp to an old tree were used to string the washing-line across the yard. But only with the Clean Air Act was there much hope that the washing would come down white.

legislation of 1963, which made private owners increasingly reluctant to rent out property at all.

For the first time, then, in the 200 years of this survey Britain faced a problem of homelessness. The issue was driven home by a BBC Wednesday Play, *Cathy Come Home*, a drama-documentary about homeless single mothers from 1966. The writer was Jeremy Sandford and the director Ken Loach, and much of it was filmed in Birmingham. For a time the plight of single mothers in hostels (now popularly known as 'Cathies') drove forward a wider debate about Britain's housing situation. The drama led to the creation of the housing charity, Shelter, and a host of equally despondent documentaries.

Meeting such growing demand created radical, but ultimately unsuccessful solutions. The new town was one such solution, but new towns contributed only a small amount to accommodation, with only 611,000 inhabitants by 1972. In addition, the centralised planning of the new towns meant that they were not always responsive to subtle changes in population trends. The early new towns, for example, assumed only low levels of private cars, with only 10 per cent having garages. By the 1960s this situation had radically altered, and places like Milton Keynes were built around the premise of car ownership. They often looked like little more than interlinked roundabouts, with little sense of community.

The position was even worse in the largest housing estates, like Cumbernauld near Glasgow and Kirby, a 750-acre former industrial estate in Liverpool. Pristine in the days of full employment, by the 1970s it was a by-word for dereliction, crime, rent arrears and vandalism. The high-rise blocks of Hyde Park in Sheffield and Castle Vale in Birmingham fared no better. Yet under pressure from central government the high-rise seemed to be the quickest and cheapest solution to the

30 A bird's-eye view of the housing revolution of the 1960s. The Castle Vale estate on what had formerly been Birmingham racecourse provided new homes for 21,000 people ousted by the mass clearance schemes. Covering 350 acres, Castle Vale was heralded as an innovative mix of houses, maisonettes and high-rise. By the 1980s, however, it had become synonymous with crime, vandalism and deprivation. In 1993 the estate was handed over to the Castle Vale Housing Action Trust and redesigned. Only two of the tower blocks are still standing.

31 'I love my new home. Where is it again?' An elderly resident settles into Castle Vale in April 1966. Birmingham's love affair with high-rise was short-lived. A report by the Department of the Environment in 1975 pronounced: 'Comprehensive slum clearance has produced incalculable psychological stress and created an atmosphere in which vandalism is rife.'

32 The speed with which Castle Vale deteriorated was remarkable. A housing scheme the size of Stratford-on-Avon lacked a sense of place or public ownership. Even by 1966, with the estate only half complete, a sense of decay and neglect had set in, as this image demonstrates.

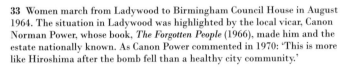

33 Women march from Ladywood to Birmingham Council House in August 1964. The situation in Ladywood was highlighted by the local vicar, Canon Norman Power, whose book, *The Forgotten People* (1966), made him and the estate nationally known. As Canon Power commented in 1970: 'This is more like Hiroshima after the bomb fell than a healthy city community.'

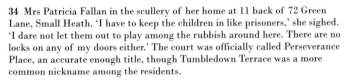

34 Mrs Patricia Fallan in the scullery of her home at 11 back of 72 Green Lane, Small Heath. 'I have to keep the children in like prisoners,' she sighed. 'I dare not let them out to play among the rubbish around here. There are no locks on any of my doors either.' The court was officially called Perseverance Place, an accurate enough title, though Tumbledown Terrace was a more common nickname among the residents.

crisis. In 1965 Liverpool was building 110 tower blocks, and flats and maisonettes accounted for 55 per cent of all tenders for local authority housing.

But the European model, rejected in the earlier years of the century, was proving no more appropriate in the 1960s. Flats were generally felt to be unsuitable for families and in need of constant maintenance, with blocked rubbish chutes and broken lifts. 'Public areas' such as passage-ways and stairwells were often vandalised and neglected, and poor construction did not help either, with complaints of high heating costs, damp and condensation. As Councillor E.J. Franklin, chair of Health Committee, said in Birmingham:

> Multi-storeys have created a human wilderness of loneliness. They have destroyed the old-style community spirit. There is an ever-growing need among people in Birmingham, particularly the elderly, to be able to talk over the garden fence.

35 By the late 1970s most local authorities had abandoned the tower-block and returned to the semi-detached. These council houses on the Hawkesley estate were part of a 1,900 house development on a green field site on the southern edge of Birmingham. They cost £12.48 a week to rent in 1978. Such housing responded to public demands for privacy, parking and porches, but swallowed up vast amounts of space.

The collapse of Ronan Point in 1968 confirmed a widespread disaffection with the tower-block, now supported by 'experts', planners and architects. When plans for the 3,000 homes at Woodgate Valley in Birmingham were drawn up in the early 1980s they were significantly different modest. There were to be no multi-storeys and 1,500 private houses were included in the scheme. Each house was to have a garage or car-port. As Alan Maudsley, City Architect claimed: 'It will look more like a private development than a municipal scheme.' What could be a greater admission of municipal failure than this?

Britain had moved a long way in the course of a century, just as the former tenants of the back-to-backs had moved far from the site of their former homes. Whether the poorer end of society were any happier or more comfortable in their new homes was another matter entirely.

FIVE

Life for Rent:
Living in the Back-to-Backs

At the beginning of the 19th century J. Blackner describes the internal arrangement of a back-to-back house in Nottingham in these words:

> The houses of the working-class, at the present time, generally consist of a cellar, a room to dwell in, called the house-place, a chamber, a shop over it to work in, a room in the roof, called a cock-loft, and a small pantry, though in the manner of building there are many exceptions, some for better, some for worse; and they are generally composed of plaster floors for the upper rooms, lightly timbered with deal; brick walls, some 4½ and some 9 inches thick; and cast-iron grates for the fireplaces, frequently with ovens and boilers of the same material.

What's remarkable about this description is how little the arrangement would change over the course of the next century and a half. True, many such houses did not possess a cellar and the workshop might well be across the other side of the court, but the central core of the building—and what it was used for—altered very little. A living room, after all, would always remain a place for living in and a bedroom (what Blackner calls a chamber) was generally a place to sleep. The introduction of services such as water, gas and (less commonly) electricity might improve the lives of the residents, but it did not alter them substantially.

But a report such as this remains cold and dispassionate. What was it actually like to live in a back-to-back? The visitors—health inspectors, midwives, rent collectors and social surveyors—can tell us much, but those who did their living there can tell us even more. This chapter, therefore, is a walk through memory as much as it is an account of official and unofficial reporting. It is based on contemporary descriptions as well as on the reminiscences of the back-to-backers themselves. There seems little need to sub-divide the chapter chronologically for exactly the reasons hinted at above. So let us enter their world.

The way into a back house was via an arched passage-way (or entry or alley or gulley or vennel, depending on the local dialect), which lay between two of the front houses. Generally speaking, there was only one passage into the court, and sometimes a wooden door at each end of it, one opening into the yard, the other onto the street. Mr Tom Foster recalls the one exception to this:

> Where two streets met at right angles there were usually two entries
> to the court on the corner, one from each street. This arrangement was
> known as a 'double knack', much loved by children since it gave an extra
> dimension to their games.

The entry itself was a little more or a little less than three feet wide. Writing of
the early 1930s Mr Foster adds:

> The narrowness of the passage gave rise to the common saying 'He
> couldn't stop a pig in an entry', meaning that he was bow-legged.
> Childhood ricketts, a dietary and vitamin deficiency leading to, amongst
> other things, bowing of the legs, had been fairly common in the preceding
> years, and the unkind jibe suggested that the pig in the entry would run
> straight through the legs.

The narrowness of the passage also made for a difficult exit if fire broke out in
the court, and coroners' reports tell of many tragedies of this kind.

The yard itself (or 'big yard' as it was called by some) we will look at later. First
we must open the door and enter one of the houses. The first sign of occupation
was a lucky horse-shoe (ineffective in most cases) above the door. As Councillor
Middlemore told the Artisans' Dwellings Enquiry in Birmingham in 1884: 'Well,
Sir, a horse-shoe is nailed over many of their doors, but it has not brought them
as yet any good luck.'

Ill-fitting or damaged doors were a bane to the life of the court families,
and a curtain—chenille, perhaps—was often hung on the inside to keep out the
dreaded draughts. The absence of anything as grand as a coat-rack meant that
coats often hung from it too, as well as the vital key to the toilet in the yard.
The room within was small, though the exact dimensions varied considerably. An
average living room was no more than 10 or 11 feet square. As a soldier tells his
comrades in the 1941 documentary 'When We Build Again': 'Try swinging a cat
in our house and you'll get whiskers all over the walls.'

The room was almost always dark, whether it was lit by an oil lamp, candles
or (generally no earlier than the 20th century) by a gas-mantle hanging from
the ceiling. The smell of the gas-light is often remembered by former residents,
as well as the popping noise the mantle made, usually just before it went up in
flames and needed replacing. The domestic gas supply was at a low level, the light
being often no more than 20 candle-power, though this did improve with time.
Nevertheless, the switch to electricity, where it did occur, was close to miraculous.
Mrs J. Mead, whose house in Small Heath was converted to electricity in the early
1930s, recalls that 'we children thought it was magic'.

The lighting of the working-class home probably changed more than anything in this period. Prior to the 1890s the paraffin lamp was still the chief form of lighting, and often remained in use upstairs even after the arrival of gas. Candles too were common, but those made from tallow provided a tempting snack for mice. It was necessary to hang them well out of harm's way. Gas itself became considerably brighter once the incandescent mantle was commercially available in the 1890s, quickly replacing the simple gas jet. Crucially for the hard-pressed household budget, it burnt less gas too.

That first impression of a room that was common to all, a kind of semi-public space, is one that visitors to the back-to-backs often comment upon, especially those who were accustomed to a sub-division of living spaces. Perhaps the most common visitor of all was the hospital midwife, despatched on her bicycle at all hours of the day and night to assist with yet another birth. One such was Olive Burns, who worked as a pupil midwife from the Sorrento Hospital in Moseley in the 1930s. She describes this first awkward encounter with the resident community thus:

> There was usually a collection of relatives and neighbours gathered in the living room; kettles were ready on the hob of a black stove, and a large teapot was on the side of the stove top. It was sometimes difficult to persuade some of the chattering ladies that their help was not required. It was also noticeable that they often related stories of difficult births in the past and 'were not sure a young nurse could cope'.

The single window did little to lift the gloom either. It looked into the interior of the yard, which was itself darkened by the high surrounding walls. Victorian social investigators almost always remarked on such sash-windows, and particularly on the brown paper with which the panes were frequently patched. Such draught exclusion—using paper or rag—suggested heroic resistance to the neglect of a landlord. Later still gelatine circles could be bought from the corner shop and stuck to the inside and outside of a window to prevent a crack from spreading. Curtains were rare in the Victorian back house, but by the 1920s we might expect a net curtain covering the lower half of the glass, and heavy draw curtains to ensure privacy at night.

Much of the centre of the room was taken up by a large table, its white wood top much scrubbed and cleaned over the years. A tablecloth to cover it was a rarity in the Victorian period. Helen Butcher recalls the attention lavished upon this single item of furniture:

> My mother's pride and joy was our table. She taught me to scrub it along the grain and, Lord help me if I started to rub in circles, I would get a punch wherever her hand made contact. Soap was not used for this type

of wood, but a slab of hard substance called bath brick. That table really
was white …

It was in such details that a family declared its aspirations and respectability. As
Stephanie Graham says of her childhood home:

> The majority of the tenants kept their homes clean and tidy and were
> quite proud of their efforts. My mother had no such pride. There were
> newspapers on the table, two chairs and no curtains, dirt everywhere, no
> bed coverings except old coats, and very rarely anything to burn on the
> fire apart from old boots, stolen from the army and navy yard next door.

The table was where meals were prepared and eaten, of course, and it stood only
a couple of feet from the range where the food was cooked. Whether there were
sufficient chairs to allow a family to collect around the table was another matter.
A single chair or a bench might be the sum total of the rest of the furniture.
Describing the living room of a Ladywood back-to-back in 1950 Sheila Gordon
comments:

> The centre-piece was usually a deal (pine) table, sometimes covered in a
> cracked American oil-cloth, which could be wiped with a dish-cloth.
> Some tenants would own an old family heirloom—a Victorian sofa
> pushed against the wall, often to hide a damp patch. It would be stuffed
> with horse hair, and the scratchy fibres would often poke through the
> worn patches and holes of the leather cover.

Unless there was a separate scullery, the table might also have on it all the crockery
and cutlery that the family owned, bone-handled knives sharpened on the front
step and a disparate collection of pottery.

If the mother of the house was engaged in out-work, or earning extra money
by making and repairing clothes, the living room was inevitably the place for this
too. Mr Foster recalled from the 1930s 'the paraphernalia of a small but busy
dressmaking business', occupying much of the available space. If, as was common
in the Victorian era, such penny industry involved chopping wood, the floor tiles
suffered in consequence.

Many Victorian landlords complained of their tenants treating their living-
room as if it were a workshop, but the evidence is not all one-sided. Investigative
journalists also testified to people's attempts—sometimes futile—to make their
house a home. Writing in 1872, one such campaigner told his readership:

> You are already familiar with the aspect of the squalid court … that it is
> smoke-dried, ricketty and dirty, that its door is a misfit, that the hinges

on its shutters are much eaten away with rust, and that one of them is broken. Entering, you are perhaps surprised to find that the room in which you stand is furnished with even an attempt at gaudiness. The cheap veneered sideboard has its collection of cheap cut-glass. The gold-framed mirror which distorts rather than reflects your face is flanked on either side with cheap coloured engravings, each of which represents a half-nude female figure. The floor is carpeted, and so is the cracked and narrow stair ...

Generally, however, the floor of the living-room was likely to be un-carpeted, at least in Victorian times, apart from a scatter of rag-rugs (sometimes called peg rugs or peg back rugs). Recycling odd ends of material or old clothes into patchwork rugs was a tradition that died hard, and one might expect to see such rugs still in use well into the 20th century. 'My mother used to buy sugar sacks to make them on,' comments Iris Hackett. Rugs served to keep down the noise, and to warm the feet, but they did not mix with the floor tiles or the linoleum (lino) which covered the house floor from the 1930s onwards, making skidding something of an occupational hazard. The rugs steadily migrated around the room as they became ever more worn and dirty—from the bedroom to the front of the fire to over the cellar grating—but they did little to conceal or deter the rising damp. Here the unfortunate residents inherited the after-effect of mass building in the early Victorian period. As Dr Robertson, Birmingham's Medical Officer of Health, remarked in 1904:

> From an examination of a number of small houses in Birmingham there is undoubted evidence that a large proportion of them are badly

36 To the children of the courts 'home-work' had a very different meaning from that of today. This image shows women and children chopping wood and tying it into bundles for firewood, and was used in the book *Women's Work and Wages*, published by Cadbury's in 1908. Almost incidental is the glimpse it gives us of the brick floor, reproduction prints on the wall, scrubbed table and Victorian grate.

37 Home-working in 1906. The woman and her son are making moulds for coffin furniture, a notable Birmingham industry. There is enough in the room to suggest a more prosperous household than many at this time. We see framed pictures on the walls, one or two ornaments on the mantelpiece and (a real status symbol, this) the presence of a clock.

38 Pearl button carding at home. Another image from the Cadbury's study, *Women's Work and Wages*, and another rare glimpse inside the back-to-back. A fast worker could get through around three cards—each of 12 dozen buttons—in an hour. But at the going rate of 3s for 14,400 buttons, it was hard to earn more than 6s or so a week, even with the whole family engaged. We see the same scrubbed table and floral wallpaper as in the other interiors.

constructed, and have unhealthy surroundings. Most of these have damp floors in the lower rooms through the tiles being laid on the bare earth. The walls are damp from the absence of any damp course, from defective brickwork and pointing, and from defective spouting.

The rising damp was often cleverly concealed behind a wooden dado, which occupied the lower part of the wall. The inside walls themselves might be wallpapered or simply painted. Jean Whitehead, writing of a period of twelve years or more in a back house in Ashted, comments:

> Towards the end of the Second World War a yellow, four-pointed star was painted by the doorways of the three cottages, indicating, we were told, that the houses were earmarked for eventual demolition. Other than a few coats of cream and green distemper indoors, the house remained in the same condition as when my parents moved in.

James Thompson, a professional house painter, was called before the Birmingham Artisans' Dwellings Enquiry in 1884, and he gives some idea of the cost of painting, white-washing and papering a back-to-back house at that date. The cost of white-washing the attic, staircase, ceiling and pantry of a three-roomed house amounted to 8s. Papering the bedrooms and kitchen added a further 7s.

> People liked wallpaper, but at times it was nailed to the wall and I have seen houses with 12 or 14 thicknesses of paper. The stench from stripping off paper is sometimes unbearable ... Even in more expensive properties of 6s a week five or six thicknesses of paper can be found.

Mr Thompson's evidence helped to explain why landlords were reluctant to re-decorate a house between tenancies. One tenant in the 1930s told a Birmingham housing enquiry that she had to remove 24 layers of wallpaper prior to redecorating.

The chief focus of the room, however, was the black-leaded range that occupied much of the right-hand wall. A typical range had a fire basket in the middle, with a small oven on each side, heated by the fire. Some ranges had a single oven and two hobs. Iris Hackett recalls her mother cooking a rice pudding in the oven 'as a special treat after Sunday dinner'. There were also occasional throwbacks to an earlier age. Mr Foster recalls as late as the 1930s 'one family who still used a clockwork turnspit in front of the fire for cooking'.

Black-leading the range was one of life's weekly chores, but tending the fire was a constant occupation, pulling forward slack and coal dust to dampen it down and prevent the coal burning too quickly. Mrs Hackett also recalls the use of a 'draw tin' or metal cover to make the fire burn more quickly, and children

were often employed to make 'butterflies' from folded newspaper to get the fire going. Still, the fire was likely to be alight all day and in most houses was the sole source of heat, and the only place in the house where the damp was kept at bay. Describing the interior of a back house in Birmingham in 1862, one journalist wrote:

> the floor is almost always wet, hot water, mostly dirty, is standing about in shallow pans, and the atmosphere is thus well saturated with moisture. It is no wonder, therefore, that there is generally found, crouching on a low chair close to the little fire, an old woman who is bent double with illness, and whose only comforts are warmth and an old short black pipe, which she puffs with a kind of resigned complacency, and which is her talisman against all the ills of this life.

Nor was it only coal that fuelled the family fire. Potato peelings headed this way too, if they were not needed for the fire below the copper in the yard. The better back-to-backs, such as those in Inge Street, had fireplaces upstairs as well.

39 2 Court, Allison Street in 1905, complete with water-pump, brewhouse and maiding-tub. The two houses at the far end of the court are blind-backs, with only a high wall to the rear of them. The image gives a good indication of the depth of the single room (around 11 feet), exactly the same as the adjoining brewhouse. The address chalked on the wall was for the benefit of the council photographer.

40 A back-to-back in Gee Street. The house was repaired by COPEC, but later demolished. The image shows many of the familiar features of a back-to-back living room: over-mantel above the range, brass ornaments, coat-hooks on the door, clothes line, suspended gas mantle, bottle of sterilised milk and a large hole in the ceiling.

Suspended on an S-shaped hook above the fire hung the family kettle, source of all tea and hot water, and boiling pretty well continuously throughout the day. The Victorian house, like any home, could be a dangerous place and it was the fire that delivered most of the fatal blows. In the living room where furnishing came at a premium, even a rudimentary fire-guard was absent, with deadly consequences to children especially. The home could be a dangerous place. Statistics from the General Hospital in Birmingham show dangers in the home, particularly from open fires and unprotected grates and especially to young children 'neglected by the mother'. Admissions for the year 1840-1 include 310 cases of scalds or burns. Two rooms at the hospital were devoted to the reception of burns and scald victims alone. In 1840 there were 53 deaths by burning and five by scalding, 21 of which were of young children. The breakdown of causes is also offered here—lighted papers, candles and proximity to the fire being chief among them.

By the 20th century we might expect a heavy fire-guard to be in place, with a set of fire-tongs and the ever-popular (and entirely useless) polished copper kettle on the hearth behind. Where a house contained young children a clothes-horse would be an almost permanent fixture in front of the fire, supplemented by clothes-lines criss-crossing the ceiling.

Above the range was often the only mantel-piece in the house, perhaps with a fringed piece of material hanging below it. Many back-to-backs, however, lacked even this. The presence of an over-mantel would be noted with appreciation and

respect by visitors to the house: it was a
sure sign of social aspiration. Here were
arranged the few family luxury items,
a clock perhaps, a vase, and a couple
of candlesticks, rarely if ever used for
the purpose for which they were made,
and often inherited. Brass ornaments,
then and now, had an odd popularity,
given the polishing that they needed.
Helen Butcher recalls that in her house
Friday was always 'fish and brass
day', when the precious heirlooms
were cleaned. Such ornaments were
becoming more common by the 20th
century. Describing *The Houses Behind*
in the 1930s Gwen Freeman writes:

> There are many ornaments on
> the high mantle [*sic*] shelves—

flowery vases which are often used as repositories for letters, money or
sweets. I have seen wax fruit, and paper and real flowers, but these are
only in the best kitchens. The art consists of family portraits, often hazy
from enlargement, framed certificates and prints from Victorian times—
Highland stags, the Infant Samuel and so on.

41 Between 1939 and
1943 the well-known
photographer, Bill
Brandt, undertook
a commission from
Bournville Village
Trust as part of a wider
debate on the planning
of post-war Britain.
The result was a series
of unique images of
back-to-back interiors
in Birmingham. The
city still had 38,000
back-to-back houses at
this date.

By the 1920s it was not uncommon for the house to have a fitted cupboard
to one side of the fireplace. Jean Whitehead describes the furnishing of her
childhood home in the 1940s thus:

> There was a built-in floor-to-ceiling cupboard in a recess alongside the
> fireplace, and another recess in which the gas meter lived. At right angles
> to this wall there was enough space for the upright piano and a sideboard.
> All the furniture, a settee and one easy chair, the deal table, the beds and
> the dining chairs, had been bought when my parents married, from the
> Times Furnishing Co. in town on 'easy terms', the only way a couple in
> their circumstances could afford a reasonable furnishing style.

The presence of a piano might seem surprising, but was not uncommon in the
Victorian or early 20th-century back-to-back, where no other source of music
was possible. The ability to play it, however, was in decline. More often than not
it became the place to store old letters or the rent book, and by the 1940s the
piano had generally given way to a wireless 'so that one may chase one Oxford

accent blaring forth from open doors all along the street', as Gwen Freeman recalls.

Well into the 1960s the gas was paid for via a coin-in-the-slot meter. Mrs Hackett recalls: 'We put pennies in the meter, which was emptied periodically by a gas man in a uniform, who carried a big leather bag to put the coppers in.'

It was the invention of the slot-meter in the 1890s that made gas a possibility for the many families who could not possibly have budgeted for a quarterly bill. This was probably when gas was introduced in Court 15. Overall in Birmingham 54.6 per cent of customers were using a meter by 1914, and the number of overall customers had risen to 172,985.

If the one side of the room followed the same pattern in almost every house, the opposite wall could vary. It was here that a scullery could be introduced (and a second window), when the house

42 Another Bill Brandt photograph from the BVT commission. The installation of a gas cooker in the living-room means that the ancient range was no longer the sole means of cooking and heating. The recesses to the side of the range were often used as cupboard space. But much as it had always been, the mantelpiece remains the preserve of clocks, ornaments and the family archives.

was modernised by the introduction of piped water and gas. Paul Lawrence, a rent-collector in the 1940s, points out that this added a further 3d a week to the 4s rent. An independent survey of tenants in Birmingham in 1934 conveyed the following comments: 'Some people said their house was damp enough without the water, and others wanted it, but had not yet succeeded in getting it laid on because others in the court would not apply for it.'

Such supplies were highly unlikely during the Victorian period, when the only source of water was out in the yard. Once connected to the mains a flat and shallow sink (a 'crock sink' it was often called) could allow some washing inside, though the tap only supplied cold water. The large family wash, however, was still more likely to be done outside in the brew-house. Not all internal sinks were connected to the mains, however. Some were 'settles' or undrained sinks. As John Nettlefold, Chairman of the Birmingham Housing Committee, remarked on the houses in the Floodgate Street area in 1905: 'There is so much trouble getting water into the house, and afterwards disposing of it as slops, that I am rather surprised to find so many people keeping themselves and their houses clean.'

43 A scullery in Clifford Street, Lozells, in 1956. Demolition was not always the immediate fate of the back-to-back in the post-war years. Such was the housing shortage that cities like Birmingham adopted a 'soling and heeling' approach in many cases. The photos taken prior to improvement give a rare insider's view of life in the courts.

When a house was connected to the gas supply (generally in the 1920s and 1930s), this was where the regulation corporation gas cooker was fitted, superseding the oven in the range. It made for a very confined space indeed, but the creation of this separate 'kitchen' (if at the expense of the living room) was clearly seen as a considerable leap in living standards.

Facing the entrance to the house were two or sometimes three doors. The first led down the cellar and invariably had a galvanised steel or zinc bathtub hanging on the inside of it. This came out on bath nights (a weekly affair) and was invariably placed in front of the fire, to be filled by the all-purpose kettle. The cellar, of course, was principally, if not entirely, for the storage of coal, which was tipped down a shute from a grating in the yard. The cellar was a dark and forbidding place, remembered with dread by many children of the back-to-backs. Mr Foster recalls: 'The cellar was always damp, and I remember that any leather items—shoes, straps and so on—that were left inside the cellar-head door quickly acquired a coating of green mould.'

44 7 Court, Price Street in 1907, complete with early telegraph pole and the ghost of a cat. Bay windows, the aspirational goal of occupants of terraced houses, were relatively rare in back-to-backs. Those seen here may well have been added during renovation of the court. So too the upper window-sills. The small windows downstairs (also added later) would have provided a little light in the scullery/kitchen.

Mrs Violet Henley, on the other hand, adds that it was a useful hiding-place from her father!

Coal did not always come down the shute, however. If the house was without a cellar, the coal was stored in a coal-hole under the stairs, and delivery meant the coalman tramping through the house. 'He looked like a miner,' recalls Mrs Hackett, 'covered in dust.' No family could survive without its coal, but small economies could be made by buying it directly from the coal-yard. Maurice Spence recalls:

> On a Saturday morning, whether it was snowing or not, I had to go down
> the coal-yard (Slater's) and get a hundredweight of coal in a pram. The
> yard was down a hill, and coming back up with the coal was really hard
> work for a ten-year-old as I was then.

Opening the second door revealed a winding and equally unlit staircase to the upper floors. The lack of a hand-rail (and the narrowness of the steps) made ascent a tricky business, and like the rag rugs the source of many a tumble. William Ridley, a relieving officer in Birmingham in the 1880s, dismissed some of the staircases as 'no better than ladders'. Sheila Gordon was a pupil midwife in Ladywood in 1950 and well recalls the difficulties posed by such stairs. She writes:

> About 2.00 am one morning I fell down one such staircase from top
> to bottom—there was no lighting—and badly sprained my ankle. On
> another occasion my generously proportioned senior midwife fell
> through a completely rotten staircase.

If there was a third door, it opened into a tiny larder or pantry, where food and crockery was stored. Despite its purpose it was certainly unventilated. Even by the 1930s not every house had a pantry, with the result that food was stored in drawers or even in the oven of the range.

At the top of the spiralling stairs lay the bedroom, with another bedroom / attic above this, if the house was a 'two-up and one-down'. Both floors could well be fitted with flimsy partitioning to create an extra bedroom for children or lodgers. 'I look on this as an attempt to live with decency,' commented Councillor Middlemore. Inevitably this would make for very small rooms, no more than five feet or so across. 'Barely large enough to have enough room to make the bed,' comments Mrs Whitehead. Her parents' room, on the other hand, had enough space in it for a washstand (there being no water upstairs), dressing table, wardrobe and her sister's cot. The marble-topped washstand became the feature of what we would now call the 'master bedroom'.

There was no part of the house where the comparative wealth or poverty of the residents was more evident than in the bedroom. An iron or brass bedstead (a specialist Birmingham product) and flock mattress suggested a family with a reasonable standard of living. Flock was a by-product of Victorian recycling, produced by tearing up and pulverising rags, old clothes, towels and discarded bedding. The Committee of Physicians who reported on Birmingham in 1843 was not happy with this kind of bedding:

> Nor do we find anything relating to their furniture or bedding that is detrimental to their health, except that the latter is often very scanty, consisting only of a small quantity of flock or feathers, the place of which would be better and more cheaply supplied by a liberal quantity of oat-chaff or straw.

But flock remained popular in spite of them. Helen Butcher has sad memories of Polly McGrath, an Irish immigrant, who worked in a flock factory in Browning Street in Birmingham in the 1920s:

> The air in the works was grey with dust from tearing cloth, and Polly worked in those conditions for eight hours each day, five days a week and four hours on Saturday morning. No wonder she died when the stuff penetrated her lungs. When the factory was burned down the glow was better than any bonfire we had ever seen.

At the other end of the scale of bedding, a mattress on the floor or (even worse) no more than a pile of rags indicated extremes of poverty. William Ridley describes people lying 'on the boards, on a mattress or on old clothes'. Even in the 1950s it was not uncommon for old coats to be used as bed covers. Sheila Gordon writes:

> I was horrified on one occasion to find the children were sleeping on naked bedsprings, with old coats spread out to lie on, no pillows, and covered with soiled grey horse blankets. It was unusual to see covers on either mattresses or pillows, and lumps of flock would be escaping through holes in the ticking, and within them possibly hordes of fleas, bugs and dust mites.

Likewise the presence of a wardrobe (always smelling strongly of moth-balls) suggested a better-off family, though again this is more likely in the 20th century. The better constructed back-to-backs had fireplaces in these upper rooms; they were a pleasant luxury, even if carrying a bucket of coal up the dark stairs was not the most welcome of household duties. Often they were left un-lit unless one

45 68 High Park Street, Nechells, in 1965. Because of the low light levels inside photographs of the interior of working-class housing are rare even this late into the 20th century. But the yard itself offers some clues. As the window-sills show, sterilised milk maintained its popularity throughout the West Midlands. Not only could it be kept without a refrigerator, it did not carry the health risks of pasteurised milk.

of the children was ill or mother was in labour. Bob Tebbet recalls an alternative way of keeping the winter chill at bay from his childhood bedroom in Lozells: 'I remember the damp and the cold in the winter, when house-bricks would be heated by the coal fire, wrapped in woollens and placed beneath the bedclothes.'

As Sheila Gordon was only too well aware, insects of various shapes and sizes were an ever-present feature of the back-to-back, residents that outstayed all but the longest of tenancies. They changed little in the course of 200 years, though few former tenants care to recall them by name. Iris Hackett writes:

> Needless to say we had bugs in the bedrooms at times. They came via cracks in the corners of the walls. They were treated with Keating's Powder, and my mom used to burn sulphur candles to kill them off. We hung fly-paper up, a long sticky tape to catch the flies that swarmed in on warm days, coming in via the dustbins.

Ironically, the making of fly-paper was exactly one of the cottage industries commonly undertaken in the back-to-backs in the 19th century.

The presence of bugs was something the back-to-backers learned to live with. Visitors tended to be more squeamish, especially if they were the health-conscious midwives. Sheila Gordon recalls:

Less obvious than the smells, but very often present, were the fleas. I learned to put my outdoor clothes in folded newspapers, which I took with me when present for a labour. After the day's visiting was over I would do a personal strip-search, standing on newspaper, and then get into the bath. Old newspapers had a very important role to play in the '40s and '50s!

Olive Burns, also working as a midwife in the 1930s, suggests that not all medical personnel were quite so careful:

Sometimes a medical student, also observing the required number of births, would arrive. He would not be wise about newspaper protection for his jacket, nor did he know the value of a piece of damp soap to catch a few stray fleas.

She goes on:

Even in rooms seemingly clean there were sometimes fleas. On two occasions, in my ignorance, I thought how untidy of the folk to put apple pips in the wash-bowl on the wooden wash-table. These brown 'pips' turned out to be like the others seen on the wall—they were bugs.

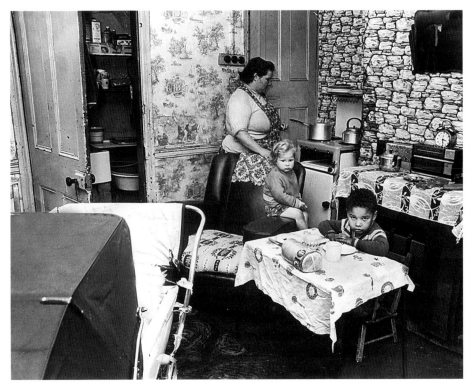

46 For those still living in a back-to-back in the 1960s, the living-room remained the place to wash and cook, store food and mind the children. The pantry in the party-wall between the two houses is similar to that in Inge Street. Such conditions in Aston were condemned in a 1969 report by Shelter, which referred to the 'waterlogged and rat-infested cellars and sewers and cisterns overflowing in the yard'.

Householders were involved in a continuous battle with bugs, spending up to 3s or 4s a week in remedies. But given the closeness of the dwellings and the perforations between them, it was almost impossible to keep them at bay for long. Councillor Middlemore lamented that 'if one house is cleansed and purified, another colony of vermin comes in from next door'. It was the common disclaimer of the back-to-backer that they were not their bugs, but ones from next door!

Again we might expect the odd peg-rug on the bedroom floor and beneath the bed a chamber-pot. This was not the colloquial name for it, of course; it was also the po, the jerry or (for more obvious reasons) the guzunder. Such an item was all that lay between a warm night indoors and a foray across the chilly yard. The pot did have to be emptied, of course, into a slop bucket or directly into the lavatory, but this was a task faced by the occupants of all houses (or their servants, at least) throughout the 18th century and much of the 19th. We would expect this first-floor bedroom to be lit by gas at some point in its life, but the supply was unlikely to reach the second floor. The first back house in Court 15 (No. 1) never had gas or electricity upstairs during all the long years of its occupation. And even if gas was provided upstairs, family economies might mean that the mantle was rarely lit, the occupants relying instead on the light from the gas-lamp in the court. One former resident remarks that it cast great shadows on the bedroom wall.

As we have said, the walls upstairs and downstairs were usually papered, even in the Victorian era, and families would make every effort to hang pictures—an old print, perhaps, or a family photograph where there were any—on the walls. The bedroom would almost certainly have a 'Bless this House' picture on the wall, or a print of 'The Light of the World'. It was, in a strange way, a Christian second line of defence to the horseshoe above the door.

Such were the delights of the back-to-backs at any time between the 1790s and the 1960s. Official reports and enquiries tended to accentuate the negative aspects of such housing, and it was clearly not hard to do so. But even here a balanced investigation heard both sides of the story. There were many who appeared before the Birmingham enquiry of 1884 to bolster the position of owners and builders in the face of an avalanche of criticism. In defence they spoke of tenants who kept chickens in their cellars and pigeons in their bedrooms, who used wood from the staircase on the fire, who made no attempt to keep their homes clean because they did not intend to stay there more than a few weeks. 'It is people who make slums,' was their refrain, a tune heard as often today as it was in the 1880s.

Those who lived there will tend to reflect more positively on the experience, though there are exceptions to this rule too. Overall they will highlight the courage, perseverance and community spirit of most back-to-backers. As Mrs Mead recalls: 'As I remember, all the neighbours were mostly friendly, which was

just as well, seeing how close together we all lived.' They will also bear testimony to the heroic attempts by mothers to keep their house and their children clean. Fathers tend to emerge with less credit in the dock of public memory. References to heavy drinking and to the squandering of household resources are common.

Reminiscence, like all history, shows the impossibility of a single point of view. Even the landlords themselves, cursed by most (if only through an agent or rent collector), can sometimes emerge with credit. Mrs Mead continues:

> … we had a very good landlord, who was a real gentleman. Every week at exactly the same time he would arrive in a limousine—the only one we had ever seen—complete with chauffeur. Every child would line up, all mothers having made sure we had a clean face, and he would pat us all on the head.

But if any aspect of the back-to-backs brings both sides together, and some degree of agreement, it was the yard and its outbuildings. It was what happened here that finally turned national and local government, and the people themselves, against this form of housing. And this is where we must look next.

47 At home in Montague Road, Long Acre, Nechells in the early 1960s. By this date the 20th century had begun to catch up with Birmingham's housing stock. Almost 95 per cent of homes now had a cold water tap, 65 per cent had a bath and 84 per cent had a toilet. But the fireplace was still the best place to dry clothes (and warm the feet) on a wet day.

SIX

The Big Yard

We met Bob Tebbet in the last chapter, carrying a hot brick wrapped in wool up to his bedroom in the 1920s. Let us briefly sit next to him on the doorstep of his house.

> I remember sitting on the doorstep looking out, while listening to my nan, mom and sister chattering away. For some reason in my memories I am variously snacking on pigs feet, tucking into soused herring with crunchy onion rings, or perhaps a bowl of rabbit stew. From my doorstep vantage point I also recall the comings and goings of neighbours in the courtyard. A blind lady (called May), always helped by another lady (her sister), as they made their way across the courtyard to the lavatory and back. And an old man (Mr Peplow), their neighbour, who sang and sometimes fell over.

Mr Tebbet's reminiscence perfectly recaptures the life of the back-to-back court, a strange blend of the private and public. Here was a world where at its most intimate—doing the family washing, visiting the lavatory—life became communal and collective. As such the rise and fall of the courtyard seems like a turning-point in English society, and historically we can look at it from two directions. From the vantage-point of the present we can observe and question a society that forced families to share what was most personal; from a position somewhere in the past we might wonder how it was that we separated ourselves so entirely from each other.

The size of the courtyards varied immensely, depending upon the number of houses that shared it, as well as the original size of the plot. In Court 15, where the back houses occupy only one side of the court, it seems surprisingly small. Many courts were never built for the number of houses that eventually filled them. But it's doubtful whether any of Birmingham's 5,000 or so courts was exactly the same as any other. In other cities, such as Leeds and Hull, the arrangement was not as a court at all, though the houses here shared facilities such as WCs and wash-houses in much the same way.

The yard was lit by a single gas lamp, or at least it was by the end of the 19th century. For the Victorian reformers, the introduction of light (ideally accompanied by air) was the first prerequisite for lifting the lives of the inhabitants. This, certainly, was in Joseph Chamberlain's mind when he argued his case before the Royal Commission on the Housing of the Working Classes in 1884. The exchange went thus:

> Still, even if the courts have gas lamps in them, these courts with a little colony getting into them, are quite apart from the general public opinion of the town; people do not go up into the court and down again?
>
> I do not know anyone in Birmingham that is apart from the general public opinion of the town, but my desire to see more lamps in the courts is dictated by a desire for cleanliness.

Such provision was unlikely to be until the 1880s, before which gas-lighting was reserved for streets, factories and the major public buildings. In 1887 only 132 courts in Birmingham had a gas lamp, and a quarter of these had been taken over by the Corporation as part of the Improvement Scheme. The 1883 Birmingham (Consolidation) Act gave the Corporation powers to force owners to install a light, and provided lamp columns and lanterns at cost price, but this did not compel them to light them. This issue (like the gas itself) generated much heat and not much light in the years that followed. But where there is a well-written Act of Parliament, there is usually a way. The Act also allowed the Corporation to adopt any court as a public highway, in which case the cornered owner would be obliged to 'sewer, level, pave, metal, macadamise, flag, kerb, channel or make good' his property.

In such circumstances, the easiest and cheaper option was to install lighting instead, and by the end of the century 3,350 courts had been provided with a lamp. The nightly ritual of lighting and extinguishing, of course, was performed by Corporation gas-lighters, who trudged an average of five miles a day to bring illumination to the town.

Yet in some parts the darkness persisted. By 1921, when the Corporation enforced the issue by installing lamps itself, there were still 1,300 unlit courts in Birmingham. We can only imagine how treacherous (and rare) must have been a midnight visit to the water-closet in such places. The switch to electricity was almost always after the Second World War. No yard in Birmingham was lit by electric light before 1939, and only 68 had been converted by 1950. Nevertheless, the Blitz was often the first stage in that change. As Jean Whitehead recalls of Francis Street in Ashted:

> A gas-lamp stood at the entrance of the big yard, which was never lit, of course, during the black-out, but was not re-connected when restrictions were ended. Its main function was to anchor a rope swing, used by all the children of the five houses.

48 3 Court, Great Colmore Street in 1904. A number of former back-to-backers refer to the presence of gardens in the courts, although getting anything to grow there was another matter entirely. The proud (and literate) gardener in this back house seems to having some success.

Also close to the centre of the yard (in normal circumstances) stood the water tap or stand-pipe, the sole supply of fresh water for the whole of the court community. Initially that supply came from artesian wells deep below the ground. Birmingham had many such wells, especially in the lower-lying parts of the town. To what extent such well water was actually used for drinking in the 18th and 19th centuries is problematic. Writing in 1848 Robert Rawlinson reported:

> Many of the wells now in existence in Birmingham, when first made, yielded comparatively pure water, and it was used for drinking and all other purposes, but at present this water can only be used for washing and scouring ...

Those who could afford it might well buy water (at a halfpenny for around four gallons) from water-carriers who hauled their carts up from the privately owned springs and wells of Digbeth. Rawlinson considered this a very expensive way to purchase water, working out at more than ten shillings per 1,000 gallons:

> ... a proper scheme of water can furnish 1,000 gallons for less than 3d, or 41 times cheaper than the carts; there is also the cost of pots or cans to hold it for use; and not the least disadvantage arising from this mode of supply is, that water kept for a few hours, exposed to atmosphere of

a dwelling-house, imbibes all the deleterious gases of the district, and rapidly becomes unfit for purposes of household use and drinking.

Here was the old 'miasma' theory on the loose again. But even setting this aside, the water cart was indeed a pricey and exhausting way of getting hold of drinking water.

An alternative source of fresh water was the town pump, free to all users. Birmingham's stood in front of St Martin's church in the Bull Ring. There was a nearer source for the people of Court 15 from the Ladywell, where the Arcadian Centre now stands. These drew from the same supply as the private wells, but from a deeper level. George Holyoake, who lived in Inge Street as a child, records that he fetched water from Ladywell 'hundreds of times' in the 1820s. His court had a pump in it, but 'we did not think much of the pump ...' Not all supplies were as convenient. The Report to the Board of Health on Dudley in 1852 noted houses in Dudley Wood where the closest source of water was a quarter of a mile away. In another court in the same area it is reported that 'the people are poor, but are clubbing their money together and sinking a well'.

But the old parish pumps, like all other underground supplies, were becoming increasingly polluted as the Victorian towns grew and industrialised. What percolated down from cemeteries, abattoirs and cesspools returned as part of the water supply. Not an ideal situation. In 1879, for example, Dr Alfred Hill, the Birmingham Medical Officer of Health, analysed 509 samples of well water and found 489 of them to be contaminated, and he reported similar statistics in the years that followed. Unwell water might be a better name for it. In such circumstances, and under the powers of the 1872 Public Health Act, property owners could be forced to abandon their wells and connect to the town supply instead. Over 3,000 wells were closed in Birmingham between 1876 and 1884.

Generally, however, we can discount water as the drink of choice. The English had long been used to taking in fluids in two other forms, as tea and as beer. The process of boiling and brewing would hopefully neutralise any dangerous impurities in the water itself. Nevertheless, a water supply was

49 A typical water-pump in a court in Rea Street. Even when connected to a mains supply such taps often leaked into the surrounding area, which might well include the back houses in the court. Rising damp and the chest infections that followed, were the inevitable result. In 1890 alone the death toll from bronchitis and pneumonia in Birmingham was 2,090, more than twice the figure for deaths from zymotic diseases.

still needed for washing, whether of food, clothes or people, and the tap in the court remained the sole source.

At some point in time most courts were plumbed into a commercial water supply, though in many cases this may not have been much before the end of the 19th century. Two such water companies operated in Birmingham in the first half of the century, before they were municipalised by Joseph Chamberlain's administration in 1875. One of Chamberlain's arguments in defence of the Bill in Parliament was that the poorer classes in the town were so destitute of water that they resorted to stealing it from the company's taps. Connection to a mains supply, however, was a mixed blessing; undoubtedly the water was purer than that coming up from the wells, but it often was not continuous. The earliest supplies in Birmingham were running only three days a week. The Romans had much the same arrangement. Only from 1853 was the water in Birmingham flowing around the clock.

50 If the weather permitted, home-work became court-work. Here three young children are chopping and bundling wood in No. 7 Court, Cheapside, in 1905. Such firewood would then be hawked in the market or streets of the town, earning a little extra money for the hard-pressed household.

By the mid-1870s Birmingham was connecting an average of 8,000 houses a year to the municipal supply, a figure that includes new houses, individual properties and courts, but the prospect of water inside the back-to-backs (other than what washed in from the court) was still very distant. As late as 1935 no fewer than 13,650 houses in the city had no mains water, and 51,794 lacked a WC.

Beside or underneath the water-pipe was a drain or, as it was often called locally, a suff. A narrow channel ran across the court towards the suff as a rudimentary form of drainage. Hither would flow all the liquids—clean and unclean—of the court. Soap-suds from the wash-house, rain-water from the roof and (least pleasant of all) liquid from overflowing pan-closets would all end up here. Many who spent their childhood in the back-to-backs will recall with pleasure their version of Pooh-sticks, racing their makeshift boats along the 'sudsy' tide that washed along the drainage channel on wash-days. There were, however, considerable risks in putting drain and drinking-water so close together, at least in the period when the supply was not piped in.

Plumbing had rarely been a priority when the drainage was first prepared. Nor, indeed, had paving the courtyard at all. Robert Rawlinson expressed a general verdict on the subject: 'The drainage is very imperfect; often the drains are choked up at their outlet so as to be rendered useless. In some courts there are good drains, but the levels are so bad that the drains are useless.'

There were also specific examples to back this up. One of the district medical officers for Birmingham described the conditions in 22 Court, Masshouse Lane, in these words:

> The drainage in this court is very bad at times; the water mixed with the ashes and filth from the dust-hole extends itself up to the court in front of the houses, to approach which to see patients I have been obliged to walk on bricks placed for the purpose, and the poor have been unable to prevent the filth from running into their houses …

This was, of course, not the case in all courts, and in most cases it was a problem perfectly capable of a solution. But the solutions did not come quickly. As late as 1901 Cumming Walters was still able to report a similar state of affairs in 2 Court, Gosta Green:

> The drainage is imperfect, and the water, instead of being cleared away, trickles down a continuation of the narrow entry which leads to yet a second yard, containing six houses, a dilapidated brew-house and partly-unroofed outhouses. The drainage here is so vile that the air seems positively putrid.

The repercussions from a blocked drain are always bad, but in the back-to-back yard they could be especially unfortunate. Helen Butcher remembers the knock-on effect in her home in Sheepcote Street in the 1920s:

> Under the house was a cellar where we kept the coal. When the suff in the yard was blocked the water would seep into our cellar. Soon the damp would rise up the walls and the snails would follow with the 'black bats' (beetles), so that the food was kept in a cupboard which hung in the living-room.

At exactly the same time, a reporter from the *Birmingham Evening Mail* was vividly describing the lakes in the courtyards of Digbeth 'from the midst of which the solitary lamp-post raised itself like a slender lighthouse'.

In some areas the problem was exacerbated by the ancient habit of keeping pigs and other animals in the yard. As the 1852 Board of Health report on Dudley says: 'Many of the people in Dudley and suburbs keep pigs' food in a sort of sunk and covered cesspool.' Pigs were, of course, excellent recyclers of household waste, and a cheap source of meat, but they are hardly the most tidy of creatures. Here again we can see a rural lifestyle transferred disastrously to an urban environment. Migrants from the Black Country and from Ireland were reluctant to abandon the tradition when they came to live in central Birmingham.

Such practices, however, were outlawed by some property owners. The Artisans' Dwellings Enquiry in 1883 was told that tenants sometimes chose cheaper accommodation in order to keep pigeons, which was not allowed in the better courts.

The position did improve eventually. From 1874 white-washers were employed to whitewash the dirtiest courts and privies, and improved sanitation, cleansing by council employees and by the tenants themselves, along with the legal obligations placed upon landlords, did serve to make the yards themselves tolerable. Those who recall their life in back-to-backs from the 1930s onwards, however critical they be about the grinding poverty of life indoors, rarely if ever complain about the state of the actual yard.

Two kinds of building occupied one side of the court. First there was the wash-house, or (as it was colloquially named in the West Midlands) the brew-house. Few would aspirate the aitch in the middle, of course. The word's origins go back at least as far as far as the 14th century, when it referred to an outhouse or room used for the brewing of ale. Chaucer uses it in this sense. By the 19th century, however, the days of personal brewing had largely disappeared, and the brew-house had another purpose entirely. It was here that the family washing was done. Not that the copper in the wash-house did duty solely on wash day. Mr Allan Gripton remembers his mother boiling all the family's Christmas puddings in their brew-house in Franklin Street.

Washing was a ritual that remained practically unchanged for the best part of two centuries. Early in the morning cold water had to be carried across from the tap in order to fill the boiler. The large cast-iron or copper container was encased in blue-brick, which helped to keep in the heat. Underneath the boiler a fire—not unlike the fire-hole in a locomotive—was started to heat the water, and wood and slack (not to mention potato-peelings and other household waste) were regularly added to keep the fire alight. Given the cost of coal, it was used sparingly here, being better employed and appreciated on the range.

Only when the water was actually boiling could washing begin. The Victorian housewife in the back-to-backs might be pushed to afford much in the way of soap, and it was unfortunate for her that prior to the arrival of Welsh water the Birmingham supply was hard and needed more soap to lather. Shavings of coal tar soap were added to the Victorian cauldron. In the 1930s a bar of Sunlight or Hudson's soap helped the scrubbing process, and adding a 'blue bag' enhanced the whites. Reckitt's starch was another essential ingredient for much of the wash. Syd Garrett recalls assisting his mother in the brew-house:

> Then I had to stir the cauldron with a piece of broom stale—promoted
> to a copper stick—so that the foamy bubbles appeared on the boiling

water. The dirty clothes were then dropped in and I was made to stir it all around … Later on, again using the copper stick, the hot, wet clothes were hooked out by the lady—too heavy for me—and dropped into a tub of water, which had been 'bucketed out' from the cauldron.

After boiling, scrubbing and starching, the washing could be removed from the boiler and transferred to a dolly-tub (of wood or galvanised steel), where a wooden dolly would be employed to get rid of the soap and to rinse the clothes in clean water. Mr Garrett continues:

A dolly or maid was used for the next job. This was a fat wooden rod, with a cross-bar handle at one end and a circular lump at the other. This wood was 'notched out', so that it resembled a miniature castle top in reverse. You then dropped the 'maid' into the tub, heavy end first, and twirled and bumped and spun it around till the dirt was bashed out of the clothes.

A mangle, also shared between the court dwellers, squeezed out the excess water, before the clothes were swilled out, put through the mangle again, and finally hung out on a line strung up across the court, typically from the gas-lamp to the brew-house. The whole procedure, especially if the family was large, could take all day. A survey by Manchester City Council in 1918 estimated that washing for a family of five took on average 9 hours 29 minutes a week.

How many such wash-houses were provided in each court varied considerably. The average seems to have been around two for each half-dozen houses, although sometimes the second building housed only the mangle and tub. Even so, a strict rota had to be observed within the court, and arguments over this were not uncommon. The *Evening Mail* reporter, quoted above, saw how frayed tempers could become on wash-day:

One woman, a broad and burly native of Ireland, was marching round the court vociferously upbraiding her absent husband, who, I gather, had not brought in the soap. In another court a band of women were squabbling vigorously for the first right to the water tap.

In such circumstances it seems highly unlikely that a whole court's washing could be done on the traditional Monday. Mr T. D. Foster comments:

My mother was always delighted when she managed to complete her washing, drying and ironing in one day, which usually meant a 6 am start. The drying needed a fine, breezy day, and a wet wash-day was a minor disaster, the only alternative being a line strung across the living-

51 Austen Chamberlain discovers an unlikely way to secure the female vote during the 1931 General Election campaign in West Birmingham. Despite the presence of washing machines and unlimited hot water, the public wash-house was never popular with Birmingham's women, who preferred to wait in line at the brewhouse. The wash-house in St George's Street, Hockley, was forced to close in December 1931.

room. The ironing was done on the living-room table, using two flat-irons heated in the fire, one in use while the other heated up.

There were two alternatives to a day spent boiling, scrubbing and hanging out in the court. From the 1860s onwards many local authorities added washhouses to their public baths, where hot water was readily available. Use of the wash-houses at Kent Street in Birmingham, which opened in 1851, cost 1d for the first hour and 1d for each additional half-hour. There were also many women who earned a few extra pennies a week by taking in washing, and returning the 'bag-wash' damp afterwards. Although the occupation 'laundress' on the Victorian censuses is sometimes taken as a euphemism for prostitute, it often meant exactly what it said on the form. Taking washing out might look like an expensive addition to household costs, but once the time involved and the cost of fuel and soap was taken into account, it was not necessarily so. A survey in 1942 found that 27 per cent of families with an annual income of less than £300 did not wash their clothes at home. Another reason for so doing was the state of the laundry. As Sheila Gordon comments on Ladywood in the 1950s: 'Another factor predisposing to the drying of clothes indoors was shame. Many of the washed articles were little better than rags, and were dried inside to hide the fact.'

And if the family's clothes were 'all they stood up in' then wash-day might be the one day in the week when the front door was kept locked! That is, if there was still a lock to lock it with. In the course of his interviews for the Children's Employment Commission in 1842 R. D. Grainger was informed by Mr Basnett, the foreman of Messrs Phipson's Pin Manufactory, that 'several of the women having only one set of clothes, and those thin and worn, were obliged on Saturday to close the door whilst they washed these things.'

The space next to the wash-houses was generally taken up by the privies. (The word 'lavatory' implies water cleansing, which was not the case for most, if not all, of the 19th century.) Again, the number of these varied between courts. Statistics from Liverpool in 1884 indicate around two privies per court, the number of houses averaging nineteen. The proportion in Birmingham was more likely to be one WC to each four or five houses, though by the 1930s the Corporation minimum was one WC to every two houses. Surprisingly this was not something the bye-laws said much about. Nor was it certain that all the lavatories were available for all the residents. If the court was being shared by a workshop or factory, then one of the lavatories might well be reserved for the workers. The toilets were always kept locked, each house having a key. It was an irony of court life that, although the houses were mostly unlocked at all times, the toilets were not.

It was the sanitary aspects of the courts that attracted more attention from the health officers and social reformers than any other. The Victorians became increasingly squeamish about such matters and with good reason. A water-closet or WC, connected to a mains sewer, was still a long way off in the first half of the 19th century, and to survive in a back-to-back court before then required a very strong constitution or a poor sense of smell. The assistant editor of the *Liverpool Daily Post* described his brief encounter with the city's Dublin Court:

> These places are cleansed and flushed by corporation employees every morning, but in the middle of the day they are always found in a disgusting and filthy condition, any other condition being scarcely possible. When we visited the place, the entrance was strewn with excrement and filth of all sorts. In all this dirt little children were playing and rolling about.

From no fault of their own the early Victorians had inherited a sewerage system little altered from the Middle Ages, where all waste—whether human or vegetable—simply lay where it was left or tipped. The medieval courts were happy to prosecute when a property owner (most famously William Shakespeare's father) blocked a thoroughfare with his dunghill, but that was the limit of their intervention. Apart from the centre of the street, anywhere—garden, gutter or yard—was a perfectly acceptable place of deposit. The huge growth in population from the middle of the 18th century onwards magnified these rural habits to an

extreme degree. As late as 1860 the Privy Council was told that in Greenock 'the common way of getting rid of refuse in houses is by depositing the contents of the chamber vessels with ashes and other filth in the roadway between the hours of 10 pm and 8 am.' Similarly Joseph Hodgson, a medical officer in Birmingham, complained in 1849 that:

> Ordure is consequently often kept in the houses, and emptied anywhere at nightfall; in other places, such as the Inkleys and other Irish quarters, the door is opened, and it is thrown out without the least reference to the spot where it falls, or anything else.

There were two main issues here: where the waste accumulated and how it was carried away, if indeed it was carried away. An improvement in one without the other was not necessarily much of an advance. In Birmingham's Hagley Road (as

52 1 and 2 House, 8 Court, Clarkson Street in 1904. The photograph shows the endless variations in the design and arrangement of courts. Here the brewhouses stand on the left and three toilets on the right. It was the responsibility of the tenants to keep the courts clean, leaving the Corporation scavengers to cleanse and deodorise the pan-closets. But all official cleaning was charged to the occupiers.

reported to Robert Rawlinson in 1849) houses were let at between £60 and £150 a year, and many had the latest in water-closets, but neither fact guaranteed what could be called a healthy environment:

> There are no drains, but open ditches on each side of the road, full of green and foetid matter. Water-closets are discharged into these surface ditches. There are cesspools on many of the premises, the overflow from which finds its way into the local wells.

But at least the cesspools were not, as far as we can judge, close to the houses. Such discrete distancing was not possible in the tightly-packed inner city. The report goes on to instance a number of courts nearer to the centre of the town:

> Yards near Three Tuns, Digbeth
> There is a close yard here with open middens and privies, with an open sewer behind, the bedroom windows open right over the open drains; one of the front houses has had fever. There is a new culvert within a few feet of this property, but the landlord refuses to drain into it.

Such was the close personal relationship between waste and waste disposal, and the earliest court privies were no more than seats which connected directly with a ditch, a cesspool or a 'dumb well'. Here the effluent remained until the authorities cleaned it out, and even then the waste only found its way as far as the River Rea. The result, related Dr Hodgson, was a watercourse 'as black as a pretty strong solution of Indian ink'.

But most vivid testimony of all was the report by a medical colleague of Joseph Hodgson, describing one of the dumb wells on the Bristol Road:

> A short time since one of these wells became overcharged, and it was necessary that it should be emptied. Men were engaged to perform this office at a remuneration of two guineas. On commencing their work the stench from the well was so horrid and overpowering that they refused to continue without a further sum of one guinea being paid to them, and a pint of brandy allowed them every hour. These terms were acceded to them, but they again withdrew from their work, and could only be induced to renew it by promise of higher pecuniary reward.

The midden was something of an advance on this, in that ashes were thrown on top of the sewage, but not a great one. The Medical Officer for South Shields described the result with evident (but powerless) disgust in 1876:

> Every house yard presents the spectacle of an enormous privy-pit, designed for the special purpose of favouring a large accumulation of

foetid refuse; its floor sunk beneath the surface, so as to ensure from its sieve-like bottom the soakage, unnoticed, of the foulest liquid into the foundations of the house.

By the early 1850s there were around 20,000 middens in Birmingham, amounting to an astonishing 13 acres of steadily decaying waste. In addition there were many ash-pits, sometimes surrounded by a low wall, where human waste was thrown and overlaid with ashes. All of these were periodically emptied by private contractors and then sold to farmers as a (very pungent) fertiliser. But Dr Hodgson reported in 1849 that there were often arguments as to whose responsibility it was to remove the waste 'till it overruns the seats, runs into the court and gives rise to noxious exhalations …' It was recognised early (at least from the time of Chadwick) that a water-based disposal system and sewer were the goals to aim towards, but the costs of that were high, and not achievable overnight.

In the meantime another form of 'overnight' action was needed. Instead of connecting directly to a midden, the privy was fitted with what was known as a 'pan-closet'. This metal pan or pail was installed under the seat and offered what was called 'closet accommodation' for a week or so, after which it was collected by nightsoilmen and a fresh pan left in its place. The dictionaries have not decided whether the term 'nightsoil' was used because the waste was collected, or believed to be deposited, mostly at night. The pan system was first introduced in northern towns such as Rochdale, and then widely adopted across the country. Birmingham adopted the pans in 1874, as part of a wider initiative in waste disposal. At the same time courts were supplied with tubs for the reception of dry ashes and vegetable matter, which were emptied at the same time. Each Birmingham van could hold 18 of the pans and a ton of rubbish from the ash-tubs.

Once fully laden, the horse-drawn vans made their way (it was not difficult to tell which roads they had taken) to what was euphemistically called the 'interception department', where the dry and wet waste were mixed together by hand and the resulting mixture sold as manure. Interception also meant the removal of rags, metal and glass, which was also sold to scrap dealers. The new system was undoubtedly labour intensive, and could only have been undertaken as part of a municipalisation of waste disposal. Nevertheless, the new system was embraced with enthusiasm. By 1884 Birmingham already had a little under 39,000 pan-closets, compared to 10,000 water-closets and 13,000 ash-pits, and the cost of weekly removal amounted to a hefty £45,000 per annum.

This official division of waste matter into dry and wet was not quickly adopted by the residents of the courts. In the West Midlands the section of the yard set aside for rubbish was traditionally known as the 'miskin'. By miskins the

1930s' residents generally meant dustbins, but this part of the yard had been known as a miskin long before anyone got round to putting bins in it. It was the refuse tip where the court's waste products were piled up.

The term was also used to describe the toilets in the yard, and this takes us back to the word's origins. The word 'mixen' is Anglo-Saxon, applied to a dung-heap as early as the 900s. By a process of letter reversal common in the West Midlands this became miskin, and survived long after its disappearance elsewhere in the country. The *Oxford English Dictionary* gives 1601 as the earliest recorded usage, but the word can be taken further back than this.

It appears in a number of Tudor inventories from Cradley Heath in the Black Country. Here the executors painstakingly listed every last item of the deceased's property, and everything of value—down to the last flitch of bacon or the dung-heap in the yard—was duly valued and entered. So the inventory of Henry Wall, who died at Cradley in 1579, includes the line: 'Item … in dounge in the miskin, valued 8 shillings'.

53 Clifford Street, Lozells, prior to improvements in 1956. The houses were provided with a bathroom and inside toilet to replace this outside one. This may be a water-closet, but the wooden surround harks back to an earlier era of sanitation. Not only was the wood subject to decay and contamination, it was also a considerable health hazard to young children. If they were able to climb onto the seat, they were just as likely to fall down it. No need, I think, to explain the presence of the newspaper.

This was a considerable sum of money, the same amount as two silver spoons in the same inventory. For the farming folk of Cradley, where there were miskins there was muck, and where there was muck there was brass. T. Fresh, referring to sanitary conditions in Liverpool in 1851, comments that until the arrival of guano as a fertiliser scavengers or nightsoilmen paid for the court's waste, rather than asking to be paid to take it away.

Back in the yard, at the business end of the new arrangement, the pan might not have looked like much of an improvement. The upper section of the toilet, above the metal pan, was of wood and likely to become stained and rotten, and sitting just a few inches above a week's supply of excrement was hardly inviting either. There were also complaints that the seats were too high and too wide for young children to use, with the inevitable result that they used the courtyard instead. 'Scores of times I have been told', reflected Dr Joseph Hodgson in 1849, '"Mind where you tred, Sir, for the children have been here!"' And ultimately, of course, the court toilet could only be as clean as the least careful of users.

But the pan-closet was in essence only a temporary measure, and the introduction of the water-closet followed fast on its heels. Not least because the Medical Officers of Health saw a direct connection between the pan-closet and ill health. In Birmingham by-laws enforced the installation of water-closets in new houses from the 1890s, and the replacement of the pans accompanied this move.

By the turn of the century more than half of the houses in the city had water-closets, even if most of them were still outside.

The impression we get from former residents is that every effort was made to keep the lavatories tidy. This was, after all, the least requirement of communal living. Mr Foster recalls the condition of the WCs in Buckingham Street in Hockley in the 1930s:

> The lavatories were always kept spotlessly clean, this being especially necessary in view of their heavy usage. Rolls of toilet paper were unknown. Instead, old newspapers torn into squares and hung on a nail were regularly used.

Tearing up the newspaper for the privy was a common childhood task, even into the 1950s.

But it was never simply the kind of closet that caused concern, it was also where it stood. James Newland, the borough engineer of Liverpool, portrayed the sanitary arrangements in his city thus:

> The houses are generally built back to back, one end of the court as a rule is either closed by houses, or, which is worse, by the privies and ash pits; or a worse state of things still, the privies and ash pits are placed at the entrance of the court, and the only air supplied to the inhabitants must pass over their foul contents.

Nor were these simply medical concerns; there were matters of Victorian decency too. Joseph Hodgson remarks on the lack of doors on many of the court privies:

> … and it frequently happens that as persons go to these privies they are obliged to pass their neighbours houses, and be subjected, more particularly the women, to the annoyance of laughing and derision from the men, and some of the women have told me, that in consequence, they have made use of the chamber-pot in their own houses and at night they have emptied it, consequently you may imagine how that is done.

Bob Tebbet recalls, at the age of four, being asked to stand guard at the toilet door while his sister was inside.

We should also bear in mind that the courts themselves were often work-places. In Birmingham workshops—what was called 'shopping'—were regularly built on top of the brew-houses and privies, a combination that was neither particularly sanitary or amenable. Court 15 had such shopping (now demolished), which the Mitchell family rented for their lock-making business, and Maurice Spence, describing life in Dymoke Street, Balsall Heath, in the 1950s, recollects the presence of a carpenter working over the brew-house in his yard. In 1888 *The Lancet* launched an enquiry into 'sweating' in the city, and as a result the Medical Officer of Health visited a number of establishments named by *The Lancet*, including two in Inge Street. He reported:

> 14 Court, Inge Street. There is ventilation on one side of the room only; the windows were open at the time of my visit. The number of people at work is seven, three men and four women. Underneath the windows are nine pan closets and a urinal, all of which are filthy and very offensive, while the nuisance from them is said to be perceptible in the workshop.

The kind of work carried out in the back-to-back yard varied infinitely. Not only were there often workshops, but families too (and especially the women) were part of a penny economy, as a means to increase the household budget. Maggie Rider remembers the various ways his mother earned extra cash in the 1920s:

> My father gave her 30 shillings house-keeping a week, this to keep a family of four to pay rent and bills. When he was unemployed or had been sacked, which was very often, she had little money coming in. Many nights she would sit up late knitting hats, jumpers, socks and other items for friends and neighbours ... Also she made toffee apples, covered first and then dipped in coconut. These were then placed upside-down on a tin tray. Local children would run up the entry to our back door and buy them for half a penny each. They were delicious.

It's clear that all kinds of personal and functional collisions were possible in this communal area, but even that did not exclude the possibility of families carving out a private space within it. Robert Rawlinson reports on fenced off yards or gardens next to the suburban cottages in Bridge Street West as far back as 1849. Mr Foster recalls the presence of gardens in the yard in Buckingham Street:

> Some of the houses in the court, though not the one in which I lived, had a small fenced-off area in front. The keener residents tried to use this patch to grow a few flowers, usually without much success since the soil was very poor. The really keen ones often tried to improve the condition of their 'gardens' with the help of the many horses which came up and down the street.

It's unlikely that any back-to-back court was designed to have a garden in it, though that does mean that residents had no access to one. In his autobiography

54 Children playing in a back yard in 1956. The back-to-back court undoubtedly provided a safe environment for children at a time when street traffic was increasing. And the resourcefulness of court kids was always evident: chalk lines on the wall for wickets, washing blue for chalk, a length of old rope for skipping and ball bearings for marbles.

55 The caption writer for this court in Stamford Street carelessly suggested a date in the 1850s. It is, of course, a century later than this, as the woman's clothes indicate, but so little had changed that such mistakes are understandable. Birmingham had begun to supply galvanised iron ash bins to its citizens shortly before the First World War in an attempt to stem the tide of overflowing rubbish. The tell-tale notice from the Estates Department on the wall suggests that this court would not be around much longer.

56 A court in Unett Street in the Summer Lane area of Birmingham in the 1960s, with some of its smaller residents. The process of 'soling and heeling' gave such houses a temporary stay of execution. However, the fenced-off garden on the left of the photograph was probably an act of unilateral annexation by the resident!

George Holyoake mentions that his grandfather owned one on the Bristol Road. 'A paradise of fruit and flowers and vegetables', he calls it. There had long been guinea gardens, small plots of land on the edge of town, rented for a guinea or half a guinea a year, upon which artisans erected summer houses and grew fruit and vegetables and, as Rawlinson describes,

> ... made them gay with old-fashioned flowers, and besides working
> in them at all spare hours, occasionally made them the scenes of
> little family festivals—the rustic arbour constructed on almost every
> allotment serving as a place for tea-drinking.

Some even took a summer vacation there. There were 250 such gardens on Calthorpe land, and others in the Rea valley at Bordesley and towards Moseley and Handsworth. The building boom put paid to almost all of thee leafy retreats, and by the 1870s all that were left were those in Westbourne Road and Chad Valley.

The introduction of gardens into the back-to-backs was generally one of the improvements carried out by (or forced upon) landlords in the inter-war years. Mrs J. Mead recalls the innovation of the mid-1930s:

> Then in 1934-35 all the courtyard surface was removed, and each house had its very own garden laid, complete with fencing and a gate. Everyone set to, and soon it began to look quite different, with flowers and a tiny lawn. We really did think that we had gone up in the world! The back strip of communal area was also altered. Every household now had its own toilet and coalhouse.

It is clear that by the middle of the 20th century the way the space in the yard was sub-divided had become very complicated indeed, but those living there knew exactly where the divisions lay. Linda Denny describes the court in Clissold Street in Birmingham where she grew up:

> In our block there were six houses. We were at the back so we had the garden, but we had to share it with the house behind us. The house to our left was a shop at the front, so they had a back yard of their own and they had their own toilet. We had to share again with the family behind us. The other toilet was for the other two houses. The toilets were at the bottom of the yard behind the gardens. Then there was an area where the miskins were kept, and next door to this was the brew-house. But the brewhouses in our yard was not used and it was all full of rubbish.

Such was the enigmatic and challenging world that lay just outside the front (or one could call it 'back') door. But for the poorer half of society (at least until the 1920s) it was the only world they were ever likely to know.

SEVEN

The Metropolis of the Midlands

The little court of houses that grew up in Inge Street was but one small cog in the wheel of a great and growing city, and the lives of those who lived there—their work and play, their hopes and dreams—only make sense as part of this wider picture. We need, therefore, to consider the world around them, and to answer the question that historians have never ceased to ask over the past 200 years. What made Birmingham grow?

In 1729 Samuel and Nathaniel Buck came to Birmingham to make a drawing of the town. They were, as far as we know, the first artists to include Birmingham in their itinerary, and the first to capture it on paper. The Bucks were full-time topographers, and their journeys around England generated a total of 89 views of the country, the earliest ones being of Leeds, Wakefield and York in 1722. By the time they reached the Midlands the Bucks' method was tried and tested: first a pen and ink sketch, then an engraving and finally a print run. The whole process took about two years. Samuel and Nathaniel were well advised to work fast, for Birmingham was beginning to change very rapidly indeed. In 1720 the population of the town was estimated at 11,400; by 1750 it had reached 23,688.

Where then should they place their easel? With the trained eye of professionals the Bucks marked their spot to the south-west of the town and looked north (see front and back endpapers). That decision would be repeated by half a dozen more landscape artists over the next 70-odd years, including the great J.M.W. Turner himself in 1795. It was not, in fact, a difficult choice: Birmingham's geography determined it. The town appeared to be shaped like a half-moon, tipped down on one side. A hill climbed up from the river along a street called Digbeth, where it met the prominent sandstone ridge running from Snow Hill in the east to Easy Hill in the west. For any skilled artist this ridge formed a natural and irresistible horizon and it was essential to make the most of it.

The skyline formed by the hill and ridge was punctuated by two dreaming spires and one tower, and as luck would have it those three buildings pretty well summarised the history of the town to that point. First there was the spire of St Martin's church in the Bull Ring, living testimony to Birmingham's ancient origins. Here lay at rest the town's medieval lords of the manor, whose ambition and economic planning had created the town and its market back in the 12th century. The Bucks' engraving caught the church before it was encased in brick and 'Georgianised' in the 1780s. At the opposite end of the horizon was the newly completed tower of St Philip's church, now the city's Anglican cathedral. Had they arrived any earlier the Bucks would have found the church still languishing in an unfinished state. Only a last minute gift of £600 by George I had allowed the nave to be crowned and completed by a suitably baroque tower and cupola.

Between the two churches, but rather closer to St Philip's in ecclesiastical sympathies, could be seen the tower of the Free Grammar School in New Street. This too had only recently been completed, as part of a drawn-out modernisation of the school. At exactly the moment that Samuel and Nathaniel were taking their measurements and making their sketches workmen were arriving to tear down the medieval guildhall, which had formed the core of the school buildings since the Reformation.

Such was the sum total of Birmingham's architectural glories, and not especially glorious ones at that. These structures aside, Birmingham resembled countless other country towns, and a considerable amount of green space both surrounded and penetrated to the heart of it. William Westley's first map of the place, published just two years after the Bucks' prospect, confirms that impression. Walker's Cherry Orchard and Corbett's Bowling Green lie between Temple Row and New Street, whilst another cherry orchard flanks the top of New Street, near to what would later be Victoria Square. The moated manor house still occupied its ancient site adjacent to the Bull Ring, and the demesne land and hunting parks of its former lords still encircled the south of the town. Beyond St Philip's only one substantial building could be seen, complete with its stately avenue of elms. Here in their Jacobean mansion called New Hall the Colmore family, once asylum seekers from the Low Countries, surveyed the town from the opposite direction to Samuel and Nathaniel Buck. No doubt they were already planning exactly what was to be done with their substantial estate.

But there was another Birmingham, one barely hinted at by Westley and entirely ignored by the Bucks. Contemporary notions of the picturesque did not permit its inclusion. One visitor to the town in 1744 was full of praise for the town on the sandstone ridge, admiring its 'new, regular streets and handsome square, all well-built and well-inhabited …' But the anonymous onlooker saw another town too, as he made his way up from the London road. 'The lower part,' he wrote, 'is filled with the workshops and warehouses of the manufacturers, and consists chiefly of old buildings …' Dr John Darwall called it a place of fever and catarrh in 1828, and added that it was 'more subject to thick fogs than higher situations'.

This lower town was indeed older by far than the one on the hill, perhaps as old as the earliest Mercian settlers in the area in the sixth century, though there is no firm evidence to prove this. Certainly it was where the market town, established in 1166 by Peter de Birmingham, had occupied the space between the River Rea and the Bull Ring. Medieval buildings still lingered here until the 20th century and one—the *Old Crown*—still survives today. Another—the *Golden Lion*—was considered surplus to requirements when Digbeth was widened in 1911 and moved to a safer spot in Cannon Hill Park. More importantly, however, the lower town was the bedrock of Birmingham's manufacturing history, and the galvanisers and welders who still occupy workshops and factory units there today are following in a metal-working tradition that stretches back at least 800 years.

Recent evidence for this remarkable continuity has been provided by archaeology. Between the demolition of the 1960s' Bull Ring and the construction of its spectacular replacement archaeologists were allowed to investigate sites in Edgbaston Street, Moor Street and Park Street during the summer of 2001. Their excavations revealed evidence, not only of substantial pottery manufacture, textile making and leather working in the area, but also of the smithing of metal from as early as the 12th century. Here was the physical manifestation of what had created Birmingham in the first place: proximity to the coal and iron deposits of south Staffordshire and a lord of the manor who was keen to encourage (and profit from) the manufacture and sale of goods at his market. Interestingly the metal being worked was already bar iron and not the ironstone itself; the Birmingham metal producers were already one step further along the industrial chain than the smelters in the Black Country.

Not all of these trades would stand the test of time. Pottery making seems to have disappeared early, but the Bull Ring's regular supply of cattle meant that the by-products of the abattoirs were still being worked in the centre of the town well into the 19th century. There was still a substantial tanning factory on Deritend in the 1850s. Such 'offensive trades' were closely monitored by the Victorian medical officers of health to make sure that they did not contaminate the food supply or unduly affect the general quality of life. The list of such industries included tripe dressing, tallow chandling, whip making, dog meat boiling, gut cleaning, horse slaughtering, blood refining and bone boiling. And this catalogue does not even include the 300 or so private slaughter-houses still operating in the town. Apart from the making of whips, however, leather working steadily slips down the hierarchy of Birmingham trades and concentrates instead across in Walsall.

There was no such slow decline in the metal trades. By the 16th century visitors to the town such as John Leland and William Camden were already being 'deafened' by the constant hammering of the smiths. In more ways than one it was already the most striking feature of the Birmingham landscape. But what was key to the town's growth and development was not simply the presence of blacksmiths; it was their specialisms. There were, after all, plenty of communities around the West Midlands—Halesowen, Cradley and Tipton among them—who hammered metal into nails and chains. Birmingham traders were working metal far more skillfully than this, into swords, knives and guns and even jewellery. Reputedly it was the sale of swords to Cromwell's army that brought Prince Rupert into the town on Easter Monday 1643, burning as he went, though Birmingham's reputation for radical preachers and Parliamentary sympathies might have attracted his attention anyway. That attack aside, the Birmingham's arms manufacturers tended to do rather nicely out of armed combat, as long as it did not disrupt foreign trade.

The Hearth Tax returns from the 1680s—a novel form of income generation by Charles II—show how far Birmingham's metal working sector had progressed by then. By 1683 we can still count 11 tanners in the town, as well as a few textile workers, but they are dwarfed by the smiths, 178 in all, and making everything from razors and knives to locks and buckles. One or two of them, in time of peace, had even beaten their swords into ploughshares. The excavations around Bull Ring testify to the increase in industrial activity around this time, but they also indicate a new range of products, one of which would make Birmingham a fortune in the century that followed. One rubbish pit in Park Street showed that bone-working still continued, generating toothbrushes, knife-handles and spoons, but it was also producing buttons. The humble button, small in itself, was to become Birmingham's greatest industry in the 18th and early 19th centuries. By 1851 more people were employed in button making (almost 5,000) than in any other single industry. As the playwright, John Home, muttered in exhaustion during his visit to the town's manufactories in 1760 'it seemed there as if God had created man only for making buttons!'

It would be hard to overestimate just how important the little button was to become. Its variety, like Cleopatra's, was infinite. It could be made from brass or gilt metal, mother-of-pearl or bone; it might be covered in linen or silk or leather; it could be decorated with glass or ivory or porcelain. It might also be the makings of a fortune. Matthew Boulton began his meteoric rise to fame at his father's button works in Snow Hill, while John Taylor, Birmingham's 18th-century king of buttons, had at his death a fortune worth some £200,000, as well as substantial landholdings and properties such as Moseley Hall and Bordesley Hall.

From the 1740s Taylor's button works were not only appealing to customers, they were attracting tourists as well. It was not simply the inexhaustible appeal of watching others at work that lured genteel visitors such as Lord Shelburne to the factory, it was the privileged glimpse into the future that it provided. Here were 500 or so men, women and children (but especially the latter two categories) at work on machines. Such machines were still hand-operated, but they immensely speeded up the stamping and pressing of the button, and the attaching of the shank to it. As Lord Shelburne reported: 'A button would pass through fifty hands, and each hand would pass perhaps a thousand buttons a day. Five times in six, children of six or seven years old do it as well as men.'

What the visitors were witnessing, of course, were early signs of the division of labour, a theory of mass production expounded by the economist, Adam Smith, who used another Birmingham industry—pin-making—to exemplify his doctrine. By breaking down the process of manufacture into a series of discrete steps, each performed by a single worker, the factory owner could speed up production immeasurably, and reduce his costs by employing mostly cheap, unskilled labour.

This technique, refined as the products and machines themselves became more sophisticated, was the trick by which Birmingham grew fat, and its application can be seen throughout the period of the Industrial Revolution. Matthew Boulton claimed in a letter to the Earl of Warwick in 1770 that the combination of 'mechanical contrivances' and 'superactive' workers enabled him to produce up to ten times the output of his rivals. John Taylor's works could produce £800-worth of buttons a week.

We can see this trick being applied across the gamut of Birmingham industries, but it can be best observed in the production of steel pens. In the 1820s the production of steel pens (strictly speaking, the pen nib) was a labour intensive business. Each nib had to be cut out individually from a sheet of steel, and this was followed by a protracted procedure of moulding, slitting and annealing before the nib was ready to use. As a result it was a costly item, retailing at one shilling each. Production was transformed by Joseph Gillott's decision to apply machinery to the process. Gillott adapted the same machines used in button-making to steel pens. From a garret in Bread Street, Gillott moved on to a workshop in Church Street, a larger workshop in Newhall Street, and finally (in 1837) to one of the first purpose-built factories in Birmingham. The Victoria Works in Graham Street are still to be seen there, though all the steel pens are now housed in a museum around the corner.

At the Victoria Works Gillott employed around 450 workers (most of them women and girls), stamping out nibs at extraordinary speed. Together they produced no fewer than 36 million pens a year, and the price dropped from a shilling each to a few pence

57 The slitting room at Joseph Gillott's Victoria Works on Graham Street. The steel pen trade was one of many industries in the city dominated by female workers. In 1891 22 per cent of brass workers in the city were female, along with 63 per cent of button makers, 92 per cent of pen makers and 95 per cent of paper bag and box makers. Not only were they cheaper to employ, they were also believed to work more efficiently than men. Such speed, of course, was helped along by the piece-work system of payment.

for a gross. All in all the Birmingham steel pen trade could turn out more than 700 million pens a year, and it's no exaggeration to say that it transformed the writing habits of the world, just at the time when literacy levels were on the rise. It has been estimated that three-quarters of everything written in the world during the Victorian era was done by hands holding Birmingham pens. At his death in 1872 Joseph Gillott's estate was worth £250,000 and his collection of musical instruments and paintings (many by Turner and Constable) fetched a further £200,000 at auction. A fellow pen maker, Josiah Mason, was somewhat more generous with his earnings than Gillott. Mason funded an orphanage in Erdington to the tune of £200,000, as well as providing property in Lancaster Street, Edmund Street, Great Charles Street and elsewhere to endow a Science College, the forerunner of Birmingham University. Nevertheless, on his death in 1881 Mason's estate still amounted to £57,000.

It is easy enough to observe and evaluate such raw capitalism from the perspective of the factory owner. The benefits for Gillott and Mason's workers, and many others like them, are more difficult to assess. As in many other industries—ammunition and brass are good examples—the steel pen trade relied heavily upon female workers. By the 1860s there were only 360 men employed in the industry, compared with more than 2,000 women and girls. And this does not include those employed (sometimes as outworkers) in boxing and packaging, who were also principally, if not entirely, female. Nor is it hard to see why. A

58 Female lathe workers in Hampton Street in 1910. The employment of women in factories during the First World War was not the cause for surprise in Birmingham or the Black Country that it was elsewhere. They had always been there. It also helps to explain why the great majority of domestic servants in Birmingham came from the surrounding counties. Girls from the city found the independence and higher wages of factory work far more preferable.

skilled woman at the top of the pen trade might earn up to one pound a week; a skilled man could pick up five times that amount. At the bottom of the heap, a young girl could expect to take home no more than about three shillings a week. This could be earned in a working week of between 52.5 and 57 hours. Samuel Timmins tells us that in 1866 the Saturday half-holiday was generally observed throughout the pen trade, suggesting therefore that workers were on duty for about ten hours a day.

There were many who found this situation distasteful, though significantly it was not the wage differentials that shocked them. Social reformers and medical experts agonised about the widespread use of women in factories, but were powerless to prevent it. Their worries were firstly that the working wife or mother seriously undermined the traditional pattern of the English family, and secondly that her health, and therefore her breeding potential, was also affected. It also seemed to fly in the face of Christian teaching. As John Angell James (the minister of Carr's Lane chapel) intoned: 'To be a good wife is a high attainment in female excellence: it is woman's brightest glory since the fall.'

To such men the factory system and female labour were anathema. Lord Shaftesbury wrote: 'It is bad enough if you corrupt the man, but if you corrupt the women you poison the waters of life at the very fountain.' And the factory, of course, was the ideal place to get one's corruption. Friedrich Engels argued similarly: 'The employment of the wife dissolves the family utterly ...' He added that 'this condition unsexes the man and takes from the woman all womanliness ...' He was supported in all this by the unions, who argued that if women could be kept out of factories, male labour would be in greater demand and wages would rise.

But the image of the Victorian family—man at work, woman at home with the children—was exactly that: an image and not a reality, at least among the working-classes. One of the main reasons for the improving finances of the Birmingham's working families was exactly because both husband and wife brought home a wage, leaving the child-minding to an older daughter ... at least until she found her way into the factory too. Such an arrangement formed the bedrock of many marriages, as the correspondent to the *Morning News* pointed out in 1871:

> Intelligent mechanics know well which class make the best wives,
> domestic servants or girls that work in factories ... Her earnings are a
> sort of dowry, and by being reckoned as part of the prospective income,
> enable alliances to be formed between boys and girls scarcely out of their
> teens. Then begins a series of shifts and troubles that will last till death,
> or mutual aversion, does them part.

Such a double income also relied, to a greater or lesser degree depending upon one's viewpoint, on child sedatives such as Godfrey's Cordial, with its heady brew of sugar and laudanum. The factory owner salved his conscience about the destruction of traditional family values by discriminating against women workers. In the pen trade and elsewhere, whereas men received a weekly wage, women were paid piece-work.

It can but strike one as ironic that many of the workers employed in the pen industry were themselves illiterate. In 1864 the factory inspector visited Josiah Mason's works in Lancaster Street and interviewed a cross-section of the children. Although the general impression is of a well-looked after workforce, the report still made depressing reading:

> Thomas Whitehouse, aged 13. At day school a month once. Don't go on Sunday. Cannot spell 'is'. Know some of my letters. Been at this and wire work since 9 years old.

> Charlotte Woodcock, aged 14. Cuts strips of steel with a rotary plane, worked by steam. Gets 3s 6d a week. Was never at a day or night school, but goes on Sunday now and then. Father or mother never said anything about school to me. Don't know 's' or 'n'.

Yet for many women and men who worked in it the factory was in marked and spacious contrast to the cramped conditions in a back-to-back house. In the 1880s James Perry's pen works in Lancaster Street covered two acres, and fronted onto four different streets. The heaviest machinery, for pressing and rolling the steel, was down in the basement, and operated by a few skilled (male) mechanics. Above were the slitting rooms and grinding rooms, lit by floor-to-ceiling windows, allowing in enough light for a job that required good eyesight. Unlike many factories the pen works had to be roomy and spacious. Near to the Corporation Street frontage was a large dining room, measuring 86 feet by 68 feet, with tables to seat 600 people. Workers could buy a hot meal here for between twopence and sixpence. At one end of the dining room was a stage, where the workers gave dramatic performances or concerts during the winter months. At the other end of the hall was a library, with around 2,000 'standard' books, which could be borrowed for free by employees.

Social reformers were prone to agonise over the indiscriminate mixing of male and female workers with its potential for immorality, but the reality at Perry's and at many more factories was that the division of labour operated along gender lines. Such arrangements can still be seen at Newman Brothers' Coffin Furniture Factory in Fleet Street. Coffin furniture was another specialist Birmingham trade, making brass and tin plates and emblems and employing around 150 workers in the 1860s. Although a customer might require fewer coffin plates than buttons, the same processes of pressing and stamping and (later on) electro-plating were applied to both. Newmans' works were designed in 1892 and closed in 1999, but the internal arrangements could easily have been witnessed a century before. On the ground floor men were employed in what was called 'hard furnishing', operating steam-driven presses and the electro-plating tanks. On the attic floor the women worked in 'soft furnishing', sewing shrouds and coffin linings. They were, in many ways, two entirely separate workforces.

Birmingham's larger factories were in general well run and well managed, but large factories were a comparative rarity in the town. Manufactories such as Matthew Boulton's at Soho (employing perhaps 800 workers) and John Taylor's might have been the most visited and reported, but they were far from the norm. Far more common were the small workshops, where no more than a handful of workers operated. Such workshops are now best preserved in the Digbeth area and especially in the Jewellery Quarter, but once spread throughout the town. The pattern of development is best explained by Samuel Timmins, writing in 1866:

> Beginning as a small master, often working in his own house with his wife and children to help him, the Birmingham workman has become a master, his trade has extended, his buildings have increased. He has used his house as a workshop, has annexed another, has built upon the garden or the yard, and consequently a large number of the manufactories are most irregular in style.

Famously it was said of a man entering the jewellery trade that all he needed to go into business was a gas jet and few old sovereigns to melt down. Of course, the remark somewhat underestimates the skill that went along with it. This Birmingham aspiration—to be one's own boss—has remained remarkably unchanged through the last three centuries. Most recently it has been embraced enthusiastically by settlers from the Indian sub-continent.

Much has been made of the positive aspects of this arrangement. For one thing a business required little capital to set up, often no more than £100 or so. For another the confrontational hierarchies of employer and employees, so often seen in the north of England, were rare in Birmingham. Other than in the brass trade, strikes and lock-outs were relatively uncommon in the city, at least until the problems at Longbridge in the mid-20th century. Partly this was due to the size of the workshops, but also the narrow dividing line—economic and social—between the workshop master and his workers. As Robert Rawlinson commented:

> It tends to a more equal and general diffusion of wealth amongst the master manufacturers, and the means of acquiring it in moderation

amongst the workspeople. There are few, if any millionaires connected with trade in or near Birmingham, if we except the Staffordshire ironmasters.

It may also explain why Birmingham was so prominently involved in the Reform campaigns of the early 1830s. Even the limited franchise on offer in 1832 seemed more of an achievable goal to workers in Birmingham than it did to many elsewhere in the country.

Great leveller though it may have been, the small workshop had noticeable disadvantages too, particularly as regards conditions of work. Not only did small workshops duck under the bar of the Factory Acts, but it was not always easy for factory inspectors to distinguish what was actually a place of work and what was simply an instance of 'out-working'. As mentioned earlier, this sleight of hand attracted the attention of *The Lancet* in 1888, which launched an under-cover investigation into such practices in Birmingham. Responding to the publicity, the Medical Officer of Health visited a number of establishments named by *The Lancet*, including two in Inge Street. Of one he commented: '45 Inge Street. This is a private house. Four people only are employed, two of who [*sic*] work in one room upstairs; three out of the four are members of the family.'

The Lancet investigators had been principally pursuing sweating in the tailoring trade, and singled out a number of English and Jewish offenders in Birmingham and the Black Country. Among the offences it noted were dangerous staircases (a feature of all back-to-back houses), shopping immediately above privies, overheating from presses, and overcrowding in shopping and upper rooms of an ostensibly private house.

> … in a back bedroom a man and two boys were at work with pressing-irons. The heat was intense. The bed lay open; the slops of the night unemptied. In another bedroom girls were hard at work. The sweater was most energetic in his protests that he kept no workshop, and that it was only his private dwelling 'mit von or two gals to help me do von leetle work just for me self.'

The positive outcome of such work, however, at least as far as the customers were concerned, was cheap clothes. One proprietor commented that he made trousers for a large Birmingham firm for 1s 6d a pair, an item that would normally have cost 5s. The price in the shop, he added bitterly, was still 20s or so.

What was true of trousers was true of so many Birmingham products. The word 'Brummagem' had been in the dictionary since the early 19th century to denote goods that were cheap and shoddy, and the term had entered the language as far back as the 1680s because of the town's reputation for counterfeit coinage.

Augustus Pugin dismissively called both Sheffield and Birmingham 'inexhaustible mines of bad taste'. Proud manufacturers like Matthew Boulton and (fifty years later) George Elkington made sterling efforts to lift the artistic level of their work, but the label took some shifting. And even they were more than happy to trade on Birmingham's tradition for 'competitive prices' and to build upon it. Both men had made great use of new technology to reduce their overheads and the cost of their products. For Boulton it had been the division of labour and the application of machinery; for Elkington it was electro-plating (patented in 1834) that allowed him to create tableware that looked like silver and gold but was (patently) not.

And thus the reception rooms and dining tables of the world were filled with Brummagem-ware. The people who bought it—from Russia to France—might not like to admit where it came from, but they assuredly liked the price. By the time of the Great Exhibition of 1851—arguably the high-water mark of British industry—half the manufactured goods of the world were made in the UK, and a large proportion of those goods originated in Birmingham. Indeed, one might say that the Exhibition itself was a creation of the West Midlands. The initial idea came after the Prince Consort's visit to the Arts and Industry Fair at Bingley House in 1849, and both the steel and the glass for the Crystal Palace were supplied from Smethwick.

As for the town itself—Birmingham did not become a city until 1889—it was unrecognisable from the one visited by Nathaniel and Samuel Buck back in 1729. If the population in the late 1720s had been nearing 15,000, by 1851 it had passed 233,000. Nor did this reflect much of an extension of the borough boundaries. In 1838 Edgbaston had been added to the borough, along with the townships of Duddeston and Nechells, and Deritend and Bordesley, but it was explosion of population in and around the centre that had made the real difference. The story of that growth can be explained from two different perspectives, from the landowners who made land available for this housing boom, and from those who took advantage of it to live in the city.

Birmingham's growth both in the 18th and 19th centuries was principally at the expense of the surrounding counties. From 1662 the Law of Settlement had prevented families from moving freely about the country in search of work; a settlement certificate guaranteed that they would return to their home parish if they became sick or unemployed. An examination of 700 such certificates in Birmingham between 1686 and 1726 shows that more than 70 per cent of migrants came from Staffordshire, Worcestershire and Warwickshire. That trend continued and grew as the century progressed. Indeed, most of the names we associate with Birmingham's history during this period—John Baskerville, the printer, James Watt and William Hutton, the town's first historian, among

59 Part of Henry Ackerman's unusual panoramic view of Birmingham (1847). This is the earliest view of Court 15, seen towards the foot of the panorama, although whether we can accept it as accurate is another question. It does suggest a surprising number of trees in the vicinity of Hurst Street, the green oasis that George Holyoake recalled from his youth.

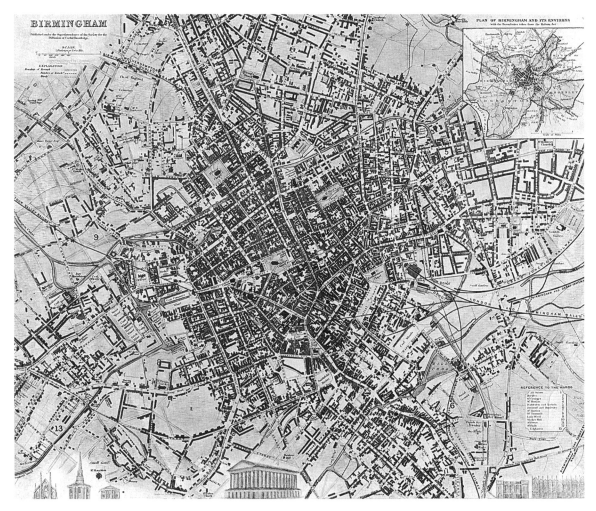

60 Map of Birmingham (*c*.1840). The canals have pushed industrial development westwards and little green space now remains in the town centre. Court 15 had just been completed at this time. The map shows a new burial ground for Jews near Bath Row (which still survives), to add to the one further along the canal.

them—were not themselves natives of the town. Nor, in the next century, was Joseph Chamberlain.

Migration, then and now, was Birmingham's life-blood. The town did not have a charter of incorporation until 1837 and though this meant that the remnants of manorial government hung on until the 19th century, it did have other, more positive aspects. No trade guilds prevented craftsmen setting up in business and no laws stopped non-Anglicans from settling and thriving in the town. As a result Birmingham became something of a haven for Quakers and Dissenters, the ancestors of families who would one day be the mainstay of Birmingham's local government and the force behind its industrial and commercial success. By the 1730s there was also a handful of Jewish traders in the town, and other migrant communities would soon be following them.

Birmingham's rainbow nation continued to diversify as the 19th century advanced. By the 1820s there was a small but growing Italian community, concentrated in the area around Fazeley Street. Such people worked mainly as itinerant musicians, ice-cream makers and sellers or as terrazzo workers. Here too were small numbers of Greek and German settlers, making use of the cheap accommodation and lodging-houses in the area. For such communities, separated from the mass of Birmingham residents by their language and religion, the back-to-back court provided the ideal environment in which to create a 'Little Italy' or a 'Little Greece'.

But by far the largest group of migrants originated from Ireland. By the 1850s almost five per cent of the town's population were born in Ireland, amounting to more than 11,000 people. Although the Irish were not concentrated in a single area like the Italians, there were nevertheless places where Irish people predominated. Slaney Street near to the Gun Quarter, Park Street (where a number of Irish lodging-houses were to be found) and London Prentice Street were three such streets. Here again the urban cottage which was the back-to-back represented a rough equivalent to what families from Roscommon, Mayo and Sligo had been used to, and in any case it was all they could afford. Indeed, many were unable to afford even this, and packed their rooms with lodgers—often extended family members or men from the same village in Ireland—to help pay the weekly rent. The names of the places they lived—Green's Village or Myrtle Row—might also suggest some rural retreat. The reality, however, was altogether more urban.

So Birmingham's population continued to grow and to widen. For many incomers it was not an easy transition. Factory work demanded rigorous hours and precise time-keeping, a system of labour entirely new to those coming from rural areas. Those used to agricultural work and 'putting-out' were accustomed to working until a job was done, not for their labour to be determined by the clock. It took a generation or more for such habits to be expunged, and factory owners from Matthew Boulton onwards railed against the tradition of Saint Monday—taking an extra day off after Sunday—among their workers. In general it was not until the second half of the 19th century that government

61 An Italian ice-cream seller in Smithfield Market in 1901. At first the ice-cream was made in the brew-houses of back-to-back courts, but stricter health controls led to purpose-built factories, which could be used by traders for as little as one shilling a week.

62 Some of Birmingham's earliest council houses in Woodcock Street. Such dwellings were well-appointed, with living-room, scullery, pantry and three bedrooms, but at 5s 6d a week were beyond the means of those who had been cleared by the Improvement Scheme. Such houses, it was argued, 'were part of the problem, not part of the solution'.

63 A waterlogged Birmingham yard as illustrated in *The Graphic* in 1876. The engravings were made at the time when many such courts were being demolished under the powers of the Artisans' Dwellings Act. Councillor White said of the area: 'The only prosperous people are the publicans. There is light and warmth in their dwellings, if not sweetness. They are the only escape of the people from the darkness of their lives.'

legislation and the introduction of steam and gas engines began to imprint a different pattern of life upon Birmingham's workforce.

The second half of the century began to change the geography of their lives too. For those economically able to escape from the inner city, ribbons of terraces began to follow the railway lines and tram routes out of town. Suburbs like Balsall Heath, Sparkbrook and Small Heath grew immensely in the 1870s, forever severing the link between home and work and creating the first generation of commuting workers.

But the story of Birmingham's growth can also be told from the landowners' perspective. It was their decisions, made at desks and in drawing rooms, that changed the horizons of all who lived in the town.

By the 18th century most of the land in and around Birmingham was owned by a small number of families. To the west lay what had formerly been the manor of Edgbaston, which was purchased by Sir Richard Gough in 1717. To the north of Colmore Row, then called New Hall Lane, was the land owned by the Colmore family. More central, but also to the south, was the former demesne land of the manor of Birmingham, which passed from the Sherlock family to Sir Thomas Gooch in 1764. The jigsaw was completed by smaller estates owned by the Inge and Bradford families, the glebe land of St Martin's church, mostly around Five Ways, and the holdings of King Edward's School. But the major developments centred upon the first three of these landowners.

It was the Colmores who made the first move, and the release of land on their estate in 1746 triggered Birmingham's building boom. Land was parcelled off and leased both to builders and directly to manufacturers, with the proviso that they erect 'one or more good and substantial dwelling houses with proper and necessary outbuildings'. For those manufacturers still occupying ageing properties down in damp old Digbeth, it must have looked the promise of heaven, and an opportunity to join the folk who lived on the hill. Substantial dwelling houses were indeed built, especially around St Paul's Square, but it would not be long before their gardens would be turned into workshops. As the leases crept further up the hill the parcels became smaller and a new industrial quarter was born to cater for Birmingham's growing army of toy makers and jewellers.

The outlook for Sir Thomas Gooch was not quite so promising. Much of his estate was close to the river, well-watered perhaps, but also liable to flooding and not ideal to build on. Indeed, when Henry Bradford released his land in the same area (on what became Bradford Street) in 1767 he let it go free to anyone willing to build there. For a century or more Birmingham's movement had been upwards and northwards, away from the Middle Ages and on to the Georgians. But Sir Thomas Gooch need not have worried. Such was the pressure inside Birmingham that expansion southwards was unavoidable, and by the mid-1760s the prices were rising fast even here. The preamble to Sir Thomas's private Act of Parliament, which permitted him to extend the leases on his land from 21 years to 120 years, used as justification 'the great want of houses in Birmingham, which hath of late years greatly increased in its trade and business, and number of inhabitants'. And so, just like the Colmore land, piece by piece, the Gooch estate was leased for workshops and houses, and this included the small patch of ground that was to become Court 15, Inge Street.

Across in Edgbaston, however, radically different decisions were about to be made. In 1786 Sir Henry Gough-Calthorpe leased the first plot on his estate. Three years earlier Sir Henry and his family had moved out of Edgbaston Hall and made for Suffolk, but the plans he had for his land were made with detailed knowledge of what was happening to Birmingham. Like a tide the crowded and industrialising town flowed down Broad Street towards the Calthorpe land, and swung around from Hockley to wash against the Hagley Road. But there it stopped. Instead of turning his estate into yet another industrial suburb, Sir

64 Deritend in c.1875. At the point where Digbeth crossed the River Rea it became part of the parish of Aston and changed its name to Deritend. The 14th-century chapel of St John has been encased in Georgian brick. The half-timbered *Golden Lion* was removed to Cannon Hill Park during road widening in 1911. Many of the street's medieval buildings were lost at this time.

Henry chose to encourage high-class residential housing instead. Lord Calthorpe would have no workshops, no 'houses of the description of labourers' or poor persons' houses', no brewshop or place of public amusement. He would allow not even a strawberry garden. Even the proprietors of the Worcester Canal were prevented from putting a tow-path on the Calthorpe side of the cut in case it attracted industrial usage or noisy traffic. If you want evidence of the power of a landowner to create an environment, the Calthorpe estate epitomises it. As Thomas Ragg commented in 1847:

> The regulations under which the Calthorpe estate is let out on building leases are such as will, for nearly a century at least, keep the parish of Edgbaston open, airy and rural. Only a certain number of houses are allowed on a given quantity of ground (always sufficient to leave good garden room), and no manufactory, taven [sic] or beerhouse is permitted to be introduced.

The result was Birmingham's Belgravia, an aristocratic and semi-rural retreat at arm's length from the town. It would be Birmingham council at home too, the chosen place of abode for the town's ruling elite, both political and industrial. Men like Joseph Gillott would move there, as well as many of Birmingham's members of Parliament. Even today the area is remarkably green and pristine, and the hanging-out of washing on Sundays is discouraged, if not actively forbidden.

The contrast with Birmingham's inner area is evident today, but it was even more stark in the 19th century. It would be possible to build a complete court of back-back houses, accommodating one hundred people or more, in the back garden of a Calthorpe estate home. Needless to say, this did not happen, and the result is as clear from the statistics compiled by the Medical Officer of Health as in the tree count. Between 1873 and 1884 the average death rate in Birmingham—at 21.4 per thousand people—was almost twice that of Edgbaston, which stood at 11.8 per thousand.

This then was Birmingham in the 13th century of its existence. The people who had poured into the town during the second half of the 18th century and first half of the 19th —both the workers and the men of property—had re-made it, as new arrivals continue to do so. It was, in most aspects, a success story, but that does not disguise the pockets of poverty and hardship that lay there too. Had there not been industry and pollution, overcrowding and disease, there would have been no need for a Calthorpe estate.

65 178-184 Newhall Street in 1904. The four properties are sandwiched between two public houses. By 1886 Birmingham had 657 public houses and 1,049 beer houses, but the number was beginning to fall. Both philanthropists and local authorities saw wages squandered on alcohol as the main reason for poverty and deprivation in the inner cities.

EIGHT

Mr Willmore's Court

On 29 May 1789, less than two months before the French Revolution, Mr John Willmore, a Birmingham builder, signed the lease for a plot of land in Hurst Street. It was not a large piece of land, measuring only 20 yards wide and 50 yards deep, but not untypical of the size of plots then being released for building. The landowner was Sir Thomas Gooch, whose land predominated in this part of the town, and whose home was in Norfolk.

We cannot, unfortunately, ask Mr Willmore what exactly he had in mind, though the lease states that within a year he was to build 'two or more good and substantial dwelling houses' and that they were to cost not less than £700. No doubt John Willmore intended to live in one of these houses. No doubt also Sir Thomas wished to ensure that this plot did not descend into the kind of multi-occupancy then beginning to appear elsewhere in the town. The lease itself was for 108 years, and the expectation of housing on the site affected the financial arrangements. For the first three years the annual rent was to be £4 3s 4d; after that it was to rise to double that sum for the remainder of the term. What the two parties were signing up to could be replicated across the whole of Birmingham, and indeed the whole of industrial England. There was a property boom, probably the biggest of the century.

The sum of £700 was a pretty good estimate. One house in Birmingham, for which the records survive, cost just over £388 in labour and materials when it was built in 1794. The largest portion of this (£140) was taken up by carpentry and joinery, followed by £118 for bricks and labour, between £20 and £25 for plastering, and £23 for plumbing, glazing and painting.

Had Mr Willmore waited a couple of months he might not have signed the lease at all. What happened in Paris in 1789 changed everything. Britain went to war with France, exports plummeted and the economy collapsed, along with the building trade. If John Willmore had been about to approach a bank for a £700 mortgage, this was probably not the moment in the business cycle to do so. By 1795 William Hutton tells us that there were 1,200 empty houses in the town, and no one in their right mind would be speculating in property. This probably explains why John Willmore's 'substantial dwelling-houses' remained words and not bricks, and the plot on Inge Street stayed empty, except for a few small workshops.

Only in 1802 did bricks and mortar finally arrive on the site. By then John Willmore was dead and his two sons, John and Joseph, were leasing the land between them. The first (and largest) house in the court—No. 50 Inge Street—was built around this time. From what survives we can imagine it as a spacious six-roomed house, with connecting doors between the front and back, and an attic running the length of the roof. A rather fine neo-classical fireplace from this time, made of timber, still survives on the first floor. But whatever its pretensions to grandeur the house had to share its grounds with a couple of nailer's workshops and what a map of 1809 calls 'horse killers'. Doubtless nailers and horse killers were the best that the Willmores could find to augment their inheritance in those difficult years.

But trade and demand do not stay flat forever. By the early 1820s the recession was over and Birmingham was expanding fast. By then, any land, no matter how small, was worth cramming houses onto, and the Willmores moved to cash in. First the large house on Inge Street was sub-divided into a front and back house, by blocking off the doorways and adding a second staircase. The division between the two was no more than a half-brick wide, somewhat compromising the privacy of the two families. The thinness of dividing walls was a perennial problem with back-to-backs. One former occupant wryly commented that her neighbours were quiet as mice, but she was kept awake by the arguments two doors down.

In the next phase another pair of front and back houses were tacked onto No. 50. Costs were kept down by having to build only on three sides, the fourth being the outside wall of the adjacent pair. Having said that, the builder was a little more generous than most. The front and back houses were separated by two spine walls, and the gap between them made room for a larder. They did,

66 Dividing the spoils. In 1796 John Snape surveyed the whole of Sir Thomas Gooch's estate in and around Birmingham, and produced a series of hand-drawn maps of his holdings. All the plots on Hurst Street were leased between 1789 and 1792; those on Inge Street were leased between 1789 (to John Birch) and 1822.

however, share the same chimney-stack. After this a third pair was added, almost identical to its neighbour, except that an arched entry through to the yard had to be included. This completed the Inge Street frontage of the court.

The range on Hurst Street was added in the early 1830s. Strictly speaking, these houses were not back-to-backs, since they did not have another row behind them, but blind-backs, one room deep and windowless at the rear. A second entry into the yard—no more than 1ft 6in. wide—was incorporated into the design. Once the Hurst Street side was finished the court was complete. Few could have guessed by then that there had once been grander plans for the site.

By this time Birmingham was well-used to back-to-backs. Among the earliest were those erected by a bricklayer called John Lewis, who built 20 of them in Queen Street and Pinfold Street in 1774. And where Mr Lewis led, hundreds of other small property owners (including the Willmores) followed. There were 15 courts in Inge Street alone.

67 Blind-back housing in 22 Court, Great Russell Street. In 1905 the Hurst Street Mission formed a Window Gardening Society, supplying seeds, bulbs and plants to court dwellers for their window boxes. Cut flowers were also distributed. 'Glad should we be,' said the secretary, 'to have the satisfaction of taking these "messengers of beauty" into the poor homes, where their cheering and welcome presence is so sadly needed.'

In 1834, when the earliest rates books appear, Court 15 was in the hands of George Willmore, no doubt the son of either John or Joseph, while Mary Ann Willmore owned Court 14 next door. George himself was living at No. 50. The first rates books do not list the occupants, but they do tell us what the estimated annual rent was from each house, ranging from £6 10s for the first house built on Inge Street down to £4 15s for the back houses. For the tenants themselves, however, it was not the annual rent but the weekly rent that was more relevant. Renting 50 Inge Street cost 2s 6d a week, compared to 1s 10d a week for one of the back houses. The first back house, which had been subdivided from No. 50, was a little more expensive, being slightly larger than its two companions in the court and having a built-in scullery. The most expensive of all the houses in the court was the one on the corner of Inge Street and Hurst Street (now called 55 Hurst Street), which rented for 3s a week. At the other end of the scale the workshop which had already been erected over the brew-house cost just 6d a week to rent.

For George Willmore all this amounted to an annual income of around £68, with the added advantage that none of his properties (being all below £10) were subject to poor rates. It would not be long before the cost of building (and the loan that preceded it) was turned into profit, especially as rents were steadily rising throughout the 1830s and 1840s. By 1840, for example, the back houses were renting for 2s 6d a week, while those fronting onto Inge Street and Hurst Street averaged 3s 4d a week. This, unfortunately, is the last date we can directly calculate the rent; from 1850 the rates books give only the rateable value.

These figures need to be given some context. In Birmingham (where wages were higher than average) a skilled male worker could expect to be picking up 30s for a six-day week, and his wife (if she was working) around 12s. Such a family would have no difficulty meeting the level of rent listed above. The average earnings of a self-employed man (as some of the residents undoubtedly were) are much more difficult to guess.

The general impression is that Birmingham's wage earners were enjoying the creature comforts that came with prosperity, a fact that those above them on the social scale were not slow to censure. A Committee of Physicians and Surgeons, for example, roundly condemned their lavish diet in 1843:

> Tea, coffee, sugar, butter, cheese, bacon (of which a great deal is
> consumed in this town) and other articles the working people purchase
> in small quantities from the hucksters, who charge an enormous profit
> on them, being, as they state, compelled to do so to cover the losses
> which they frequently sustain by bad debts. Huckster dealing is a most
> extravagant mode of dealing; there were in this town in 1834 717 of these

shops, and the number has increased greatly since that time. Meat is purchased in the same improvident manner; the working men generally contrive to have a good joint of meat upon the Sunday; the dinner on the other days of the week is made from steak and chops, which is the most extravagant mode either of purchasing or cooking meat.

'Improvident' is the key word here. Steady, comfortable earning was never enough. In an age in which being out of work—through old age, unemployment or sickness—meant being out of money, there were poverty traps lying in wait for all. As Councillor Middlemore told the Artisans' Dwellings Enquiry in 1884:

> I have found old men getting lower and lower wages as they get older
> and older, until at last they receive only a boy's remuneration, and I have
> found wives and daughters nobly supporting their crippled fathers and
> husbands.

Among the better paid and more provident workers there were saving schemes, such as building clubs, sick clubs, burial clubs, watch clubs and clothes' clubs to meet such eventualities. Saving could begin at Sunday School, but by far the majority of such clubs were based in pubs. As William Sanders told the Select Committee on Friendly Societies in 1849: 'There are about 1,700 public houses and beer shops, and it would be near the mark to say that two out of every three have one of these societies, and some have five or six ...'

Many other clubs (around 500) were based in factories, where members paid 3d or 4d ever Saturday night. Dr John Darwall estimated in 1834 that there were 800 such clubs in Birmingham, and there were well over 1,000 by 1849, with strange and revealing names like Modern Druids, Nelson's Friendly Sick Society, Society of Total Abstinence, and Old Women's Society. Membership of a sick club allowed the member to choose and change a surgeon, and to receive medical attention when he or she needed it 'instead of losing their time and aggravating their disease by begging for hospital or dispensary notes, or endangering their lives by resorting to druggists or domestic remedies ...' Unfortunately for the membership, friendly societies and clubs often folded, and then the safety net was well and truly cut. It was said in 1849 that over half the male paupers in Birmingham Workhouse were there because their club had broken up. And here—at a stroke—the provident were levelled with those whom the Victorians called 'the residuum', or 'the submerged tenth', those unable or unwilling to set aside something for a rainy day.

The rents in Court 15 were above average for back-to-backs at this time. No doubt this partly reflects the better standard of the houses and the smallness of the court. But it may also be because the front houses (and some of the backs) were already being used for trade. The 1841 census (the earliest which includes names of occupants) shows us a butcher, Richard Biddle, living at one of the Hurst Street houses, with a carpenter called Thomas Wiltshire next door. The latter, in fact, was less of a house and more of a furnishing department; Mr Wiltshire had with him as lodgers two apprentice cabinet-makers, and an apprentice painter. It is one of the many cases where the occupations of Court 15 perfectly reflect the economic demands outside.

It is not a simple task to recover the rest of the court because the 1841 census does not allocate house numbers. But comparison with the 1840 rate book does allow us to reconstruct the Hurst Street side with some confidence. Thomas Wiltshire the carpenter lived at 55 Hurst Street with his wife and son and the three apprentices. All aged 20 years, the three young men would have been approaching the end of their seven-year apprenticeship. Richard Biddle, the butcher, was at 57 Hurst Street and there are two lodgers, a 14-year-old boy working at a brass foundry and a hawker called Samuel Leonard. No doubt the latter plied his trade down at the Bull Ring, where there were legions of hawkers. At 59 Hurst Street George Holdcroft made coach frames, again with a younger man working for him. At 61 Hurst Street there is a Jewish man by the name of Pascoe Aaronson. He was around 80 years of age (the 1841 enumerators round up ages to a multiple of five) and was or had been a surgeon. Finally, at 63 Hurst Street, lives Isaac Harris, who may also be Jewish, since his children are named Jacob, Henry and Deborah, although his wife is called Catherine. Isaac's house was a general shop, and would remain so for a century and more.

Who was living in the front and back houses on Inge Street is not as easy to establish. The rates books for 1840 describe 52 Inge Street as empty, but by the time of the census in following year there were occupants, the first appearance of a family who would be still be living in the court almost 100 years later. Thomas Mitchell hailed from Wolverhampton, and it's not surprising that a man from this centre of the lock trade should have as his profession cabinet lock-maker. Thomas and his wife, Ann, were in their 30s and already had four children, the youngest of whom was just two months old. We know from the children's baptisms that the family must have moved from Wolverhampton to Birmingham between 1829 and 1832, but not immediately into the court. Nevertheless, Thomas Mitchell junior was probably the first child to be born in Court 15. Who knows how many more would follow in the next 130 years?

The occupations of other residents, when we can tie them to the court, suggest traditional crafts, but ones which could be pursued at home. There was a mangler (washerwoman), another carpenter, a cabinet-maker, a joiner and a dyer. In most cases we could say that Court 15 was home to a community of skilled artisans. What seems most striking about the court at this date is how crowded it is. There appear to be 61 people living in the 11 houses. This is partly the result of large families (two families have five children), but also of shared occupancy. Having a lodger was one way to make up the rent, and even better if he happened to work for you. No doubt one of the first tasks pursued by the carpenters was to put partitions up in the bedrooms.

By 1841 the population of the borough of Birmingham had reached 177,922, almost two-thirds of whom lived in the central wards. R. D. Grainger, who reported to the Children's Employment Commission in 1843, claimed that there were 2,030 courts by 1838, with a total of 12,254 houses, and he estimated the number of people living in courts at 49,016. But it's clear that the population was still rising fast. As the *Birmingham Journal* reported on 21 January 1854:

> During the first fifty years of the century, the average increase was 608
> houses, with above 3,000 of a population per annum; for the ten years
> ending 1851, the increase in houses was about 500 every year, with an
> annual augmentation of the population of nearly 5,000 … In the last
> fifteen months ending March (1853), the increase in houses was 3,020,
> equivalent to an augmented population of nearly 15,000 persons in this
> brief space of time.

The article goes on to herald the forthcoming provision of a free library, baths and parks and a system of sewerage costing £150,000, 'making Birmingham not only the cleanest, but the best drained and the most healthy town in the kingdom …' Mr Grainger too was relatively upbeat about Birmingham's domestic and industrial conditions. There was, as yet, little evidence of the overcrowding and sub-letting that would eventually become a part of court life, at least in the poorest districts. 'Each family has generally a separate house to itself; the hours of work are moderate; there are no large and crowded factories such as abound in the cotton districts …'

Grainger similarly argued that separate housing and the court system had contributed to the comparatively good health of the town and its freedom from major epidemics. It is ironic that exactly the opposite argument was being used by the health reformers of the 1870s.

As part of his tour Mr Grainger visited the house of a pearl button-maker, the family consisting of father, mother and one grown-up daughter. His description gives us a rare insight into the domestic world of the better class of artisans, such as those who lived in our court:

> The house is neat and tidy and consists of four rooms. The father
> earns, at good work, 18s, but the prices are very much reduced, which
> is attributed to the work of men being done by women. The mother

68 28 Court, William Street in 1904, after reconstructive surgery. The widespread Victorian belief that the introduction of light and air would lift the lives of the court dwellers led to what were called 'Nettlefold courts' in Birmingham. The demolition of one or two sides of the court (and the addition of bay windows) created miniature terraces and a much improved environment. A total of 91 such courts had been opened up by 1908.

can read a little, the daughter was taught to read and write; went to a day-school till 8 years, and to a Sunday School till 12 ... The house is well-furnished and has altogether a comfortable appearance. There are sufficient kitchen utensils, candle-sticks, and spoons; a metal soup ladle was on the table for dinner, which consisted of meat, potatoes, and bread. A clock was in the adjoining room. The house is situated in a court, but this is large and spacious, being towards the outskirts of town. The rent is 3s 6d.

J. Pigott Smith, Surveyor to the Street Commissioners, was equally up-beat about the recently-built houses, such as those in Inge Street. He was, however, much less enamoured of the older courts, and particularly of the state of their sanitation:

The courts on the whole are tolerably spacious, especially those newly built. In the older parts of the town a branch drain is in many instances carried from the culvert in the street up to the pump in the court; in

PLAN OF
BIRMINGHAM
TAKEN IN THE YEAR
1731

SCALE OF YARDS.
SCALE OF CHAINS.
SCALE OF 4 FURLONGS OR HALF A MILE.

other instances the water is conveyed over the surface in an open drain into the street, and thence under the footpath into the culvert. There are very few courts in which the water lies stagnant. In each court there is usually a pump; in some instances 1 pump serves for 2 courts. In many cases water is supplied from the Waterworks Company. There is a wash-house in each court for common use. As regards the privies, there are generally 2 or 3 in each court ... These are often in a filthy state and immediately join each other. When the privies are emptied, the soil is wheeled into the street and immediately carted away; but as the nightmen are sometimes negligent, some remains are occasionally left and constitute a serious nuisance.

There were additional problems in some of the older districts. Robert Rawlinson commented that the arrival of several railway lines in the 1840s—the London & Birmingham, Birmingham & Derby, Grand Junction and later the Great Western—had taken out much property in the inner area without providing alternative accommodation for those needing to remain in the centre for work. 'In some instances the consequence has been injurious overcrowding by parties taking rooms in occupied court houses.'

If we move on to 1851 the census tells us that 57 people were living in Court 15. Of these 36 were born in the West Midlands (including Wolverhampton, Coleshill and Atherstone). One of the occupants did not know where she was born. Many of those born in Birmingham were children, their parents originating in places as far afield as London, Wales and Yorkshire. As such, the make-up of the court reflects the overall Birmingham statistics. A total of 8,277 people in the town were born in Ireland, 3,582 were from London and 1,227 from Wales. First generation Jewish settlers are included in the overseas figure, which is only 642. By far the largest figures, however, are for those born in the West Midland counties of Staffordshire, Worcestershire and Gloucestershire (and, to a lesser extent, Herefordshire and Shropshire). A combination of higher wages, availability of work and domestic service were continuing to draw people into the town from the neighbouring counties.

The 1851 census allows us to reconstruct the court with much more accuracy than in 1841. At 1 House Sophia Hodson and her three eldest children were pearl button makers, whilst at 3 House Charles Nation and an unrelated lodger (John Foley) were steel toy-filers. At 53 Inge Street (a street house) Francis Foster and two of his sons were wire workers. It seems unlikely, though not impossible, that they were working from home. It's likely that Thomas Mitchell, listed with his eldest son as locksmith and bell-hanger, may well have been working in and out of the court.

69 Pigott Smith's map of Birmingham, surveyed in 1824-5. This is one of the few contemporary maps to indicate land-ownership, and shows the extent of the Gooch holdings in the south of the town. The River Rea is in most cases the southern boundary of the estate.

Sophia Hodson's trade can be paralleled with Catherine Holyoake (George Holyoake's mother), a horn button maker, whose outworking is described in George's autobiography:

> My mother had a workshop attached to the house, in which she conducted a business herself, employing several hands. She had the business before her marriage. She received the orders; made the purchases of materials; superintended the making of the goods; made out the accounts; and received the money; besides taking care of her growing family.

Her husband, George Holyoake senior, worked at the Eagle Foundry across the town.

It may well be that the remaining properties, particularly those fronting Hurst Street, were both retail and domestic. At 57 Hurst Street Richard Biddle was still trading as a butcher, as he had in 1841. At 59 Hurst Street Edward Kingham probably worked and traded as a brass ornament and letter cutter, whilst at 61 Hurst Street George Duke was working in leather, making saddles and collars. Finally, at 63 Hurst Street, Lawrence Levy was trading as a watch maker, not an unusual trade for a Jewish man. In fact, so sub-divided and specialist had Birmingham industry become that Lawrence was actually making only the hands of clocks and watches. His two sons, Joseph and Morris, are listed as apprentices. It seems likely that Lawrence had apprenticed his sons elsewhere in order to hone their skills. It is probable that 52 Inge Street was also a shop—a tailor's—an occupation that continued in the court for more than 100 years. Given the area, we might have expected the owner to be Jewish, but Thomas Williams is Welsh. Hardly any of the tradesmen and women is working alone, which fits the pattern of outworking elsewhere in the city. We do not, of course, know about others working in the court who did not sleep there on the night of the census.

Various features suggest a relatively prosperous court. The sons of two families are apprentices, indicating higher aspirations and relative wealth, while the Duke family (61 Hurst Street) have a domestic servant, though one wonders whether the servant was employed elsewhere. They also have a lodger. During the extensive renovation work on 1 House, an early stencil pattern was uncovered on the walls of the ground-floor room, which has now been reproduced on the same walls. This too suggests that the earliest occupants were relatively well-off.

Sophia Hodson, who lived at the back of the Levis, has an interesting story to tell on her own. Born in Coleshill, she reflects the trend of moving from rural to urban life. Her maiden name is James, and her mother, Elizabeth James, is living as a widow in the house. If the ages given for her children are correct, Sophia's eldest child was born when her mother was 15 or 16 and she was a widow

70 The living-room of 1 House, reconstructed as the home of the Levy family in the 1840s. An original stencil pattern found on the wall has been reproduced. The house had its own scullery / kitchen, the entrance to which can be seen to the right of the door. This was probably built originally only as a food-store, the sink being added at a later date.

71 Birmingham Domestic Mission Hall in Hurst Street. Established in 1844 (and rebuilt in 1870), this was one of a number of missionary organisations in the town taking the Christian message to its darkest corners. The missionary's report of 1892 says of one visit: 'Household consisting of father, mother and two daughters. Father out of work, mother lying dead, and daughter lying ill in the same room.'

by the age of 27. Whether Sophia is working from home is not known, but the presence of her widowed mother must have solved any child care problems. Still, a house of seven persons (there are eight in the Fosters' household) must have been crowded.

Sophia was one of few women in the court who was in paid employment, though as a widow she had little choice in the matter. Even in Birmingham, where female working was common, there were moral and logistical difficulties in doing so. Speaking to Grainger, the partner of one button firm claimed that educated men (earning 18s to £1 a week) rarely allowed their wives to be employed at manufactories, with a consequent improvement in domestic cleanliness. They also sent their children to Sunday School regularly. Grainger also attributed the high death-rate among infants under five to the tendency of women to work 'until the very day of their confinement, and to return to work three weeks later'. Jemima Toules, one of the interviewees, told him:

> The infants are left in the care of little girls as nurses, or with female
> relations, as the grandmother, if there be any, or are put out to
> neighbours; pays herself 2s 6d for her child, this includes washing,
> but no food. Infants are fed by the hand whilst the mothers are at work.
> Godfrey's Cordial or 'something to sleep them' is often given.

The presence of the Levy family, and Pascoe Aaronson ten years earlier, highlights the fact that Hurst Street had become the centre of Birmingham's Jewish community. There had been Jewish traders in Birmingham since the

1730s, and the earliest trade directory (Sketchley's, 1767) lists eight, including Mayer Oppenheim who had a glass-house in Snow Hill. By the 1850s there were 140 families, making a total of some 730 people, rising to 3,200 people by the end of the century. The enumerator's books indicate a wide variety of origins for these people, but the majority were Ashkenazi Jews fleeing from pogroms and discrimination in Poland, Prussia and Germany.

72 The three back houses and yard of Court 15 during reconstruction work. The bay windows of 2 House and 3 House were not part of the original design, but inserted into the frontages around 1900. Both were subsequently bricked up. The sash windows above, however, still retained their original glazing.

The little community first set up in the Froggery, a low swampy area now buried underneath New Street Station. William Hutton tells us that the Jews took over a small house there with a garden at the side, pulled down the interior wall and built a synagogue, using the garden as a burial ground. There was another burial ground in Granville Street, also lost to the railways. It was a poor community of mainly hawkers, whom Hutton calls 'the drooping ensign of poverty' and 'the remnant of Israel'. This notion of travelling for a living, with Birmingham as a base, was still partly true by the 1850s.

But for most of the 19th century it was the area around Hurst Street, Inge Street, the Inkleys, and Smallbrook Street that was the centre of the Jewish community. A synagogue was built in Hurst Street in 1791, and the foundation stone of a Hebrew National School in the street was laid on 9 August 1843 by Sir Moses Montefiore. Jenny Lind, the Swedish Nightingale, sang a benefit concert for the school in September 1847. The courts around Hurst Street were well adapted as havens for a particular community, or people sharing the same language. Inge Street had whole courts populated by Russians or Poles. Often settlement began as lodgers on the top floor of a house owned by an earlier migrant. Asher Rosenberg housed 12 Jewish lodgers in Bath Passage in 1851, all glaziers or tailors, whilst Harris Belcher in Gooch Street had five carpenters from Poland in his house, as well as seven children.

When Robert Rawlinson visited Birmingham in 1849 for the Board of Health he was struck by how 'many of the men work in garrets at their own houses, and have several boys under them'. What was happening in Court 15 seems to support this. In the back house next to Sophia Hodson lived Charles and Emma Nation and their two sons. Charles was a steel toy-filer. This was a common enough Birmingham trade and one that could be carried on at home. The fact that the fifth member of the household—a lodger called John Foley—was also a steel toy-filer also seems to indicate that the little house was a workshop as well as a home. So too at the third back house, where Thomas Williams the tailor and his family lived, and no doubt were helping him with his tailoring. Robert Williams, a journeyman tailor who was present on the night of the 1851 census, may only have been visiting his relations, but equally could have been assisting in the business.

Rawlinson also counted 2,600 different occupations in the town, carried out in rooms or factories or independently in their own homes, and Court 15 gives us a microcosm of this remarkable range. In the Hurst Street houses dwelt a locksmith and bell-hanger (the Mitchells were diversifying), a butcher and milkman, a brass ornament and letter cutter, a saddle and collar maker, and three watch-makers. In Inge Street there were a cordwainer, a shoemaker, a pearl button maker, two wire workers and a brass founder's apprentice, in addition to those mentioned above in the back houses.

The Report of the Children's Employment Commission (1843) also refers to the beneficial effects of diversity of trade. 'It rarely happens that all the members of the same family work in the same trade, so that if one trade is in a depressed state, another may be in thriving condition.' The son of Richard Biddle, the butcher, for example, was working at a brass foundry in 1841 and in a warehouse ten years later.

Such was the state of Court 15 in the middle years of the 19th century. Trades came and went, as did the occupants of the 11 houses, but our overall impression is that life was treating the court well. Birmingham had welcomed these strangers and given them jobs, and chance had made them neighbours. Their houses were relatively new, and if the plumbing (or lack of it) left something to be desired, pretty much the whole of the town was in the same (leaking) boat. But times change, and life for the next generation in Court 15 would not be quite so rosy.

NINE

Hawkers, Tailors and Glass Eye Makers

By the 1880s the environment around Inge Street had changed much, certainly since George Holyoake had lived there in the 1830s. To him it was now 'a dead street': 'Inge Street now, looking down from the Horse Fair end, is, as it were, the entrance to a coal-pit, which, when I first knew it, appeared as the entrance to a sylvan glen.'

The area was now thoroughly commercial and the range of shops was wide. In Hurst Street businesses ranged from those presumably servicing the local area, such as tobacconists, fruiterers, butchers and bakers, to those with a wider market such as whip makers, sign writers, chair caners and blacksmiths. Proximity to the markets seems to be indicated in the number of businesses specialising in leather (whips, boots, saddlery) as well as butchers and bone turners. In Inge Street tailors' shops predominated, as well as glaziers, two professions which tended to be dominated by Jews.

Tailoring remained an unbreakable thread in Court 15 too, though not with a Jewish connection. Back in 1851 Thomas Williams had been using 52 Inge Street as his house and shop. Ten years later James Williams (a relation, perhaps) had taken over the tailoring business and moved into 50 Inge Street. The bigger rooms at No. 50 would have been useful, since James and his wife had six young children: William, Gwen, James, John, Maud and Jessie. More intriguing still, the Williams family had taken over not only No. 50, but the house next door as well. Internally there is no sign that the two properties were 'knocked through', suggesting that the one house was used for trade and the other for living in.

But stability was not something the Victorian families of Birmingham enjoyed for long. After 1861 James and Ann Williams had two more children—Lydia and Joseph—but they served only to replace the two youngest girls, who died in infancy. Their father too had died before the 1871 census, by which time Ann was carrying on the tailoring business as a widow. By then her two oldest children—now in their 20s—had moved away. And here (at the time of the 1871 census) we can see how fluid and flexible the houses in a back-to-back court could be. Ann Williams and her four children lived only at 50 Inge Street, whilst another family, headed by Francis Hill, were occupying both 51 and 52 Inge Street.

Francis Hill's profession reflects a new and growing trade in the town. He was a gas fitter, no doubt working for one of the companies installing street lights in the area. Perhaps he even fixed up one for the court. Francis hailed from Dudley, but had spent more than half his life in Birmingham, married a girl from London and they shared the house with four sons and two daughters. Mr Hill's salary might have been stretched for a family of eight, but there were three other wage-earners in the house. One son was employed as a bellows maker and another (at the age of 13) was working as a japanner. A daughter was employed as a polisher, no doubt in one of the many brassworks.

The municipal take-over of the gas undertaking three years later does not seem to have unduly disrupted Francis Hill's career path. By 1881 (now aged 63 years) he had risen to the grade of lamp inspector. The family itself, however, had undergone considerable changes. Mrs Hill had died and only two of the children were still living at home. Thomas—the bellows maker—was still there, along with Mary, who had since married and now had a young daughter herself. Not that the rest of the family had moved far. When William Hill, one of the other sons, tied the marital knot, he and his wife had moved into 3 House at the back of the court.

There are two ways of judging the relative poverty or affluence of a court such as this. One is obviously the rateable value of the properties, which is in turn reflected in the rent the tenants were paying. The other is the length of time tenants stay there. Occupiers with little or nothing in the way of personal effects moved often, and found it easy to do so. Victorian landlords expected their poorest tenants to remain no more than a few months, which gave them ample opportunity (though seldom the inclination) to redecorate a house two or three times in a year. As one house agent, Thomas Grimley, told the Artisans' Dwellings Enquiry in 1884:

> A respectable artisan's dwelling, if it did not change hands, ought not
> to need cleaning more than once in three years; but it was seldom that a
> house was occupied for so long, so that a landlord had frequently to do
> a house up half-a-dozen times in a couple of years.

In such circumstances the slow blinking flashlight of the census, illuminating only once every ten years, is a less than useful research tool. That said, it is all we have. But even the census shows that Court 15 is different. This may partly be because houses were also used as businesses and, once they had fitted out their rooms as such, the occupiers were less likely to leave. The Williams and Mitchell familes show this, but so too does one of the most intriguing families in the court, the Oldfields.

We first meet the family in the 1861 census, when 1 House was packed to the rafters by Herbert and Ann Oldfield and their eight children. Herbert Oldfield originated from Uttoxeter in Staffordshire, but it is not easy to trace his steps

73 A street party in Lozells, Birmingham, for Queen Victoria's Diamond Jubilee in 1897. Interestingly the party consists entirely of women and children (and one dog). The picture was kept as a postcard by the current owner's grandfather, James Parker Woodbridge. The kind of housing seen here combines both the sense of a court community and the independence of the terrace.

much further back. Herbert gives the names of two entirely different men as his father on his two marriage certificates. The implication, perhaps, is that he was illegitimate. Parish records show that Herbert and Ann married at All Saints' church in Birmingham in 1839, when Ann was just 18 and her husband five years older. Since that time Ann Oldfield had been pregnant roughly every two years. But defying Birmingham's poor record in child mortality, only one of the ten children—Matthew—had died in infancy (from laryngitis) in 1846. Strangely to us, a second son was also christened Matthew just four years later.

But it is Herbert Oldfield's employment that makes life inside 1 House especially interesting. On the 1861 census Herbert declares his profession as 'glass worker'. Such work, of course, could have been pursued in a glassworks (of which Birmingham had a number, particularly around the canal basin on Broad Street), but his listing in the 1871 census as 'bead and glass toy maker' and as 'artificial eye maker' in the 1881 directory indicates a workshop, making the glass eyes for dolls, toy animals and stuffed animals. He may even have made artificial human eyes.

Birmingham's endlessly flexible labour market had cornered the market even in this trade. Not only were wild birds re-deployed as wall and table ornaments, even the city's vast population of cats and kittens (bred in the courts to keep the rats at bay) found their last resting-place in a glass case. One manufacturer in Broad Street employed his whole family in the grim business of stuffing kittens as pen-holders, wall-mounts or arranged in costumed groups. Such kittens' tea-parties have long since been relegated to museum basements, but in the mid-19th century occupied many shop windows and cabinets of curiosity. And all required the careful and constant work of a glass eye maker.

Other than the Mitchells, Herbert Oldfield is the only worker in the court at this time to advertise in the trade directories, and we can also imagine a sign on the wall in Inge Street, summoning clients down the alley to seek his services. Here they would have found Mr Oldfield blowing his glass and blending the strands of colour. Herbert would have kept in the house trays of glass eyes of various sizes and pigments for his customers to choose from.

Herbert spent the rest of his long life in Court 15. Ann Oldfield passed away in 1872, but Herbert re-married five years later, which given the size of his family was probably a wise move. But Sarah Brown, Herbert's second wife, was already in her 50s and not in the best of health. She died just two years later in 1879 from (as the doctor at the General Hospital described it on her death certificate) long-term heart disease and bronchitis. Herbert lived on as a widower for a further 18 years, and was still making his glass eyes into his 80th year. Sadly his was not a profession (or an age) in which money could be set aside for a comfortable retirement. Herbert died in 1897 in the workhouse infirmary in Western Road from 'senile dementia and exhaustion'.

Our lives are measured out in certificates, and those from the Oldfields comprise a large bundle, charting the family from cradle to grave, and from Court 15 out into the suburbs of the city. Such was the rate of dispersal and death that when Walter Oldfield died in the court in 1893, it was not his father or a sibling who was present at his death and reported it to the registrar, but a neighbour from 2 House. This was the close-knit world of the court, in which births and deaths were shared as readily as cups of sugar.

By 1881, when Herbert and his son, Alfred, were sharing the business, there were some 41 people living in the 11 houses of the court. The Mitchell family were still occupying 55 Hurst Street (the corner house), though it is now headed by Benjamin Mitchell, the son of Thomas Mitchell, who presumably had died between the 1871 and 1881 censuses. The family continued to trade as Thomas Mitchell & Son some years after his death. From 1861 onwards the Mitchell family were occupying both 53 Inge Street and 55 Hurst Street, which were adjoining houses. It again reflects the fluidity in the house boundaries. In 1891, for example, Alfred Shanks, the butcher, and his wife occupy both 2 House and 3 House in the court. It has to be said, however, that the census enumerators probably found the internal arrangements in the court as confusing as we do, and may easily have got the exact details wrong. Benjamin Mitchell and his family probably moved across to 55 Hurst Street on the death of his father, while Benjamin's brother, James, now occupies 53 Inge Street. The whole family is still engaged in lock making, and that tradition has now been passed on to Benjamin's son as well. James Mitchell is listed as a key maker. He remained at this house for at least 20 years and never married. The rates books show that the Mitchells were also using the shopping over the outbuildings from the 1840s into the 1930s.

In contrast to his erstwhile neighbour, however, Benjamin Mitchell made sufficient money to escape the poverty trap. On his death in March 1907 Benjamin left an estate worth £1,718, and the presence of a will (a rarity indeed for those connected with Court 15) affords us a glimpse into the superior lifestyle he enjoyed at 359 Rotton Park Road in Edgbaston. Not only did he have a servant (as we would expect of a house of this size), the more accommodating rooms of Rotton Park housed a piano and a walnut chiffoniere. These last two were bequeathed to his daughter, leaving the rest of the furniture, plate, glass, books and pictures to his wife. There were also gifts of £50 each to his brothers, James and Thomas, who lived on in the court.

By this date the Hurst Street frontages were firmly established as retail premises. John Rose at 57 Hurst Street, though listed as 'painter pressman' in

74 Aerial view of central Birmingham (1959). Pershore Street runs north through the middle of the photograph and crosses Bromsgrove Street towards the top. Despite the obvious signs of site clearances a number of blind-back and back-to-back courts can still be seen near the foot of the picture. The photos were taken in order to identify traffic congestion.

the census, is named as shopkeeper in the 1880 (and later) trade directories. Next door at 59 Hurst Street Eliza Wheeler calls herself a gin dealer on the 1881 census and a china dealer in the trade directory, and has a servant to help. Unusually, this servant called Esther Bevan is 61 years old. 61 Hurst Street does not appear in directories until 1894, when it is occupied by Albert Mountjoy, who sweeps chimneys. We should probably call it a commercial property, rather than retail. In 1881 William Manton lives there with his wife and two young sons. Manton is an upholsterer, perhaps mending and re-covering furniture. One wonders whether he is related to Elizabeth Manton, who ran the *Black Lion* two doors down the street. More intriguing still, William Manton was born in the United States, but the reason for his appearance in Birmingham is not known. 63 Hurst Street does not seem to be in commercial or retail use. Rosina Hakersley, her son and one of her daughters, are employed in Birmingham's extensive metal trades: in screws, brass and door knobs. Her older daughter is a French polisher.

By the 1880s it was becoming much more difficult for families to use their children as supplementary wage earners. Legislation had blocked off a number of options. Attendance at an elementary school up to the age of 12 had become compulsory in 1880, while some school boards such as Birmingham's had made attendance compulsory in 1871 for children aged between five and thirteen. The fact that schooling was not free only compounded the problem. Initially charges stood at an average of 2d a week for children under seven and 3d for children over seven. In 1876 a standard charge of 1d was introduced. Legislation had also increased the age at which children could work in a factory, and the delicate balance between school leaving age and factory age was not easy to maintain. It was said in the Factory Inspector's report for 1890 that many children reached the exemption standard at 11, too young by two years to work full-time in a factory. Rather than being sent to work as half-timers: '… children become errand boys and girls until the age of 13 years. They thus get into idle habits, are learning no useful trade or handicraft, and run great risks of getting into mischief.'

In 1881 the youngest worker in Court 15 was George Ellis, who at the age of 14 was employed as a corksock maker. Contrast this with the 1871 census, where Rosina Hackerley's son, William, was working as an errand boy at the age of eight years. That said, we cannot trust residents to be entirely honest in declaring the employment of their children to the enumerator.

There are a number of features of the court in 1881 that are distinctive and different from the earlier generation. Firstly, there is the absence of what we might call the nuclear family. In five of the 11 houses the head of household is a widow or widower, the youngest (Eliza Wheeler) being just 34 years old. In contrast, however, we can clearly see evidence of the extended family. Three generations share 52 Inge Street and 63 Hurst Street, whilst in-laws are present

75 The Hurst Street side of Court 15, with the tower of the Hippodrome theatre behind, in 1953. Worthington Tours took over 65 Hurst Street in 1946, and the company's car park extended around the rear of the court, taking advantage of the demolition of adjoining properties. The 1950s were a profitable time to be in the holiday business, and Mr Worthington had franchises in hotels in Switzerland and Austria, as well as the UK. In wet weather the proprietor's chauffeur drove him the 100 yards to the barber for his morning shave.

76 The Hurst Street frontages in 2004. Eliza Wheeler was briefly the tenant of 57 Hurst Street, next to the corner shop, in the early 1880s. Successive trade directories describe her as a china dealer and fruiterer, but on the 1881 census she declares herself to be a gin dealer. At that time she was 34 years old and a widow. Her place of birth was Ludlow in Shropshire.

in three more households. Overall, the court has undoubtedly aged. In 1851 there were 18 children not listed as in employment; by 1881 this number has fallen to nine. More than anything this accounts for the drop in numbers living in the court.

Almost certainly the economic standing of the court had dropped since the 1850s. The two boarders (usually a sign of difficulties meeting the rent) are in low paid jobs: fish hawker and bone turner. The Oldfields could certainly accommodate a lodger, since their house had once held nine people. Some indication of the drop in value of the properties until the mid-1880s (and therefore of the economic standing of the occupants) can be gleaned from the rates books. After all, the court was now 50 years old, and a number of the houses much older still. Surviving rates books show that rateable values (our only indication of rent after 1850) slowed or even fell until the later 1880s, after which they begin to rise steadily again. Unfortunately it is impossible to convert rateable value directly into weekly rental, but we know that a similar court in Fisher Street had back rents at 2s 1d and front rents at 3s 10d. But we must be wary of tying rateable values too closely to rents. The 1884 Housing Enquiry was told that rents in the town had fallen over the past few years, but had been rising seven or eight years before that.

The properties on Hurst Street, and the front houses on Inge Street, are always rated somewhat higher (usually by about £1 or £2 per annum) than those at the rear. There is, however, a considerable hike in the rateable value of the Hurst Street houses between 1886 (when they average £6 15s.) and 1896 (when they are valued at £16 10s.). This seems to reflect their new designation as 'retail shop and house', as opposed to 'house and premises' as they are called earlier. These properties may well also be benefiting from the introduction of a gas supply.

One strong reason for the declining status of the inner city courts was an economic exodus. The people of Birmingham, so long restricted to the central wards of the town, were now spilling far and wide across the surrounding areas, all of which would be subsumed into Greater Birmingham in 1912. Once independent villages such as Harborne and Handsworth saw their populations double between 1861 and 1901, leaving an ageing and dwindling housing stock in the town centre. One of the positive benefits of this was that the population of the central areas was thinning out. In his statement to the Royal Commission on the Housing of the Working Classes in 1884 Joseph Chamberlain testified that Birmingham was not overcrowded, with an average of 49.4 persons to an acre, compared with 108 in Liverpool, 85 in Glasgow and 79 in Manchester. Overcrowding was said to affect only 2,082 people in the town.

Those able to move to the new suburbs—typically, white-collar workers such as clerks, shopkeepers and teachers—were able to afford the additional transport costs on top of higher rents. Front houses in Ladypool Road in Balsall Heath cost 6s and back ones 5s, and perhaps half of these households were also able to afford a general servant. The form of their new houses was determined by the model by-laws of the Local Government Board (adopted by Birmingham in 1876), which laid down a minimum air space on two sides between properties. The suburban result was bye-law houses and bye-law streets, all of regulation size and width and consisting of vast numbers of terraced or tunnel-back houses. But while the suburbs resembled a vast building site, in the town centre the rate of house construction dropped, from almost 3,000 a year in 1876 to less than 1,000 a year in 1882.

As we have seen in Chapter 2, national legislation also empowered councils to address the problems of inner-city housing. Birmingham's first clearances took place on the site of the proposed railway stations at New Street and Snow Hill in the 1840s and 1850s, followed by demolition around the site of the Council House in Edmund Street. The Artisans' Dwellings Act of 1875 led to the major Improvement Scheme of 1875-82, covering 43 acres of the town centre, when many of the gullets and courts of St Mary's ward were cleared away to allow for the building of Corporation Street. The estimated cost of the scheme was almost £1.5 million, a third of which would be borne by the ratepayers. The Corporation did not, at this time, take it upon itself to build replacement housing. As Joseph Chamberlain told the Royal Commission in 1884:

> It really consists almost entirely in making provision for the destruction of unhealthy and overcrowded dwellings, and the reconstruction and re-housing of the poor may safely be left to private enterprise.

Nevertheless, the Corporation did eventually enter the housing market itself. The earliest council housing was in Ryder Street and Lawrence Street (near to what is now Aston University) in 1889-90, when a total of 104 artisans' dwellings were erected at a cost of £182 each, with rents of 5s 6d. In Milk Street, off Digbeth, a series of two-storey flats was completed in 1901, with artificially low rents of 4s 3d on the ground floor, and 3s 9d on the first floor. But the move towards flats (the central platform of Birmingham's housing programme in the 1950s and 1960s) and the pressure to expand the housing area of the city outwards into the suburbs (a key idea of the 1920s onwards) were still the subject of intense and sometimes acrimonious debate in what seemed to be a endless line of public enquiries.

The nature of the evidence presented at such hearings was not always uncontested, and the allegation was made that exceptional cases were sometimes cited as general examples. Councillor Middlemore's evidence to the Artisans' Dwellings Enquiry Committee (1884) was criticised by Joseph Chamberlain for

77 Front houses and corner shop in St Martin's Street. The chief deterrent that prevented families from moving house was the dreaded 'key money', a sum paid to the landlord on taking up a tenancy. The charge survived well into the 20th century, when it was usually described as a deposit to cover redecoration and repair. Key money might amount to half a week's rent.

this tendency. Yet Councillor Middlemore's vivid evidence is worth considering; it may not be directly applicable to life in Court 15, but it is to the worst of the back-to-backs. Among many examples he cited:

> ... the case of a man and his wife living in a kitchen 12 feet by 10 feet, where the woman had lately been confined, and where seven other also slept, and where the baby, to quote the poor mother's words, had 'just died by the will of God and Dr Jones'.

Reform meant changing the hearts and minds of the middle and upper classes, and in consequence the councillor's comments are directly pitched into the gulf that lay between their experience and those who lived in the neglected heart of the inner city:

> If, for example, he were compelled to stable some of his thoroughbred horses in the houses in question, I think he would enter a vigorous protest against such accommodation and communicate with the Society for the Prevention of Cruelty to Animals ... Now, Sir, what is the general condition and habits of the poorer inhabitants, that is, the majority of the inhabitants of this [St Mary's] ward. Well, Sir, a horse shoe is nailed over many of their doors, but it has not brought them as yet any good luck. They are very much what circumstances have made them. Music,

which brightens every house in Edgbaston, has been excluded from
their lives; so has beauty, and so has knowledge; so too has all healthy
rejoicing ...

In the worst cases houses were being rented for up to 4s a week and then the
furnished rooms sub-let to labourers' families for 5s a week. This sub-letting was
more often done by the tenant than the landlord, and involved only the outlay
of £1 or so on some furniture. This world of the truly impoverished dominates
the evidence presented in the housing enquiries of the 1880s, and it makes grim
reading. Councillor Middlemore reports:

> In another three-roomed house I found the kitchen and attic were
> occupied by a man, his wife and three children, and the middle room by
> a black man and a white woman—the former of whom gets his living by
> selling religious literature.

In some of the poorest districts, it was said by the MOH in his annual report
for 1884, tenants had sold or burnt the woodwork from the doors, staircases,
window-frames and ash-tubs, and sold the boilers and drain covers for scrap
metal. Officials found it difficult to accept that the British economy itself could
be the cause of such distress and tended to blame the demon drink instead:

> As to drunkenness, I found a very large number of women with black
> eyes a few days after Christmas, many of whom seemed to regard a black
> eye as part of the Christmas festivities ... In some streets—Sheep Street,
> for example—one woman in every four or five seemed to have a black eye.

The reluctance of landlords to undertake repairs is also frequently condemned
in the enquiries, but it is defended too, not only by the landlords but by poorer
tenants as well. Intervention or prosecution by the Health Committee served
only to reduce the income from property, and to push up rents. In one case cited
the elderly tenant, resident for 40 years, was paying a weekly rent of 2s. 3d. out
of a wage of 14s. A rise in rent, or the forced move to a more expensive house, it
was argued, would serve only to send him to the workhouse. The house agent who
gave evidence to the Artisans' Dwellings Enquiry suggested that a house with a
3s. rental cost 35s. to 40s. a year in repairs. The income from a court such as that
in Inge Street amounted to no more than £175 p.a. Once the rates and mortgage
were paid, the profit from this piece of capitalism would not have been large.
J.H. Loughton told the Artisans' Dwellings Enquiry that if the remaining lease
on property was short, the owner would be reluctant to spend money on repairs.
There was more money to be made, said the urban missionary attached to Carrs
Lane, from lodging-houses than from courts.

One of the factors driving the great housing debate forward was the increasing availability of statistics on health and mortality. Birmingham's record on health might have been better than comparable towns such as Manchester and Liverpool, but it was not good. During the 1880s around 45 per cent of deaths were of children under the age of five years, and 43 per cent of all deaths were due to zymotic diseases, and infection borne by water, air or food. Cholera, typhus and typhoid were particularly virulent, but so too were measles and diarrhoea, and many deaths occurred from secondary infections or dehydration in individuals (especially children) weakened by poor diet or primary infection. In the eight most insanitary streets in the Improvement Scheme area, the annual death-rate was 53.2 per thousand, compared with a city-wide average of 21 per thousand in 1883. The death-rate among children was much higher. In 1900 it was 199 per thousand and was estimated to be up to 300 in certain streets.

The death-rate can also be broken down into wards and was used to underline that the further people lived from the centre, the greater their life-expectation. In 1900, for example, the death-rate in St Mary's ward (in the city centre) was still 29.7. Moving towards 'the fringes' in Market Hall ward it had fallen to 16, and to 13 in Harborne and Edgbaston. The zymotic diseases are blamed for much of this, but so also is consumption. As Dr Alfred Hill, the Medical Officer of Health, reported in 1901:

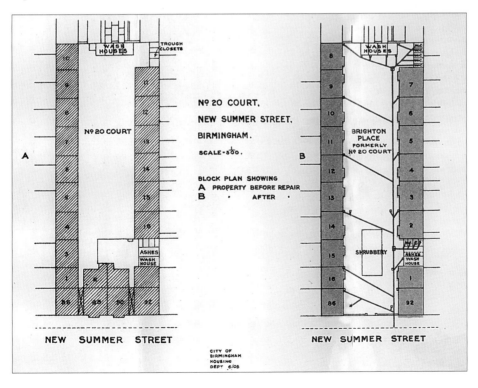

78 The conversion of 20 Court, New Summer Lane, into a 'Nettlefold Court' in 1903-5. The 22 houses in the court have been reduced to 18, the trough or pan closets converted to WCs, and a raised shrubbery placed where a brick wall had been earlier. And as a final flourish 20 Court has now been triumphantly re-branded as Brighton Place.

79 Mr Arthur Bingham behind the counter of his sweet shop in the late 1940s. Mr Bingham retired from the business in 1966, but 55 Hurst Street remained a sweet shop for a further five years or so. Much of the trade came from patrons of the Hippodrome theatre across the road, and the shop stayed open to catch the evening performances.

It is impossible for the germs of consumption to live in fresh air and sunshine, and therefore it is important that the working population, at any rate, should maintain their physical standard by getting outside and obtaining that fresh air and sunshine which is so essential to their health.

Medical care was, of course, beyond the reach of many and they resorted instead to the patent medicine vendor shouting his wares in the Bull Ring. In 1880 the reporter for the *Daily Globe* parodied the kind of patter often heard in the shadow of Nelson's statue:

This liddel lozing is gombosed of honey, horehound and hysop, it will relieve a goff or gold immediately, at once ... Now if any gentleman is droubled with a goff, I will give him a leedle lozing that will gure him at once.

It was no wonder that the most popular sweets sold at the sweet shop on Hurst Street were troche drops, menthol and eucalyptus, and bronchial pastels.

How well-off were the families in Court 15? It is not an easy question to answer. One thing we can say is that many working-class families in Birmingham were in a rather better position than those in the north (where the wages were lower) or in London (where rents were higher). In 1884, for example, a skilled cabinet maker, bricklayer or carpenter could expect to earn around 30s a week, and a goods' clerk or porter around 20s. Out of this, weekly rent of 6s or 7s would be paid. At the 'Housing of the Working Classes' debate in 1901 it was said that in London a man would spend a third of his wages on rent; in Birmingham this was more like one fifth.

A series of articles in the *Morning News* in the 1870s gives a good indication of how far such a wage would stretch. The expenditure is for the family of a 'decent Birmingham mechanic'. This is for husband, wife and four children, and therefore includes 10d a week for the as yet compulsory 'schoolpence'. The list is broken down into food (at 19s per week) and other essentials including rent, clothes, fuel and household items (at 13s 7d), a weekly sum that would have put most working families with one breadwinner into the red. The household items include blacking, firewood, tapes and cottons and the replacement of broken crockery and brushes. The food estimate is based on a daily diet of:

> Breakfast: Tea or coffee, with bread and butter or toast spread with lard or dripping
>
> Dinner: Meat and vegetables
>
> Tea: Same as breakfast
>
> Supper: Bread and cheese and beer
>
> The children might have boiled milk and bread for breakfast, and the dinner might be varied one day in the week with fish. Sunday might be celebrated with a pudding.

By the 1880s Birmingham families were benefiting from the import of cheap food (bread from the US, meat from Australia), which helped to reduce the cost of living. Nevertheless, the cost of food certainly took up a larger proportion of family income (around 60 per cent) than it does today.

But not everyone enjoyed the income of a 'decent mechanic'. The housing debate of 1901 was told that '35 per cent of the general population of our city's toilers earn wages which do not exceed one pound a week', and in these circumstances Birmingham's poorer citizens had to use considerable creativity in their shopping. *The Morning News* supplies a comparative list for a family with a widowed mother and son, where the family combine wages to meet costs of 13s a week. Here the diet consists of little more than daily bread, butter or lard and tea, with a hot dinner only on Sundays. On lower wages the housewife might be buying: 'the fibrous, withered stuff that goes by the name of beef and mutton in the cheap butchers' shops ... hideous lumps of indigestible bullock's liver and rusty bacon and granitic cheese ...'

The provision shops in the poorer areas tended to be very general in their stock, as a reporter for *The Daily Globe* describes in 1880:

80 A Conference on Christian Politics, Economics and Citizenship, held in Birmingham in April 1924, led to the formation of COPEC, a society dedicated to the improvement of housing in the city. The row of back-to-backs (and derelict pub) in Gee Street was purchased and demolished in 1935 and replaced by flats and maisonettes. For the first time in their lives the residents were provided with electric light.

A little, old bow window: the panes of glass, some nine inches by six in size, are patched with brown paper neatly pasted over the cracks and holes; the window frames are rotten and white from lack of paint; very dirty old newspapers of a date long gone by cover the bottom of the window … Then the stock! A few ends of rusty bacon … a skinny, dried haddock, one or two consumptive-looking bloaters, a few withered vegetables, a few onions putting forth luxuriant sprouts, a few oranges … an assortment of pickles, boot-laces, sweets, blacking and matches …

The later Victorian period heralded the rise of the fried fish shop, which also sold trotters and pickles, in the poorer districts, as many as one to twelve frontages in some streets. The trade directories, however, show only one such shop in Hurst Street in the 1880s and no increase until after the First World War.

The Morning News chronicles how easily the family could spiral downwards when the breadwinner was put out of work, stopping payments into a sick club, pawning household items such as the clock, the change of linen, the bed, and having to borrow from the employer from the following week's wages (a system known as 'calf'). The coalman, it was suggested, might charge a higher price when his coal was not bought for ready money. The huckster too thrived in such a situation, being willing to sell goods on tick, but at a higher price than shop price. And so the downward spiral continued.

Wages were generally paid on Saturdays, which in many factories was a half day. For a lot of families, therefore, Saturday evening was the time to redeem

81 Allen's Cross estate at Northfield. Built in the inter-war years, such estates offered semi-detached tranquility at between 10s and 16s a week. But there also had to be room in the family budget for transport costs. The journey into the city centre involved a bus trip of three-quarters of an hour, followed by a tram journey of 20 minutes. Estates like these provided eager customers for the motor cars being manufactured at nearby Longbridge.

items from the pawnbroker's. This shuttling to and from the pawnbroker became an elaborate dance around unpaid bills, debts and needs. Saturday evening was also the best time to buy the week's food (and Sunday's roast), when the traders in the Market Hall or Fish Market began to drop the price of their perishable stock. The wholesale meat market at Smithfield, which supplied most of the city's butchers' shops, was opened as a retail market on Saturday nights, selling off what had not been taken up by the butchers. The beef, mutton and lamb was not of good quality, but it was cheap, at 6d a lb for lamb, from 4d to 7d for beef and less for mutton. Cheaper still was offal and rabbit, which was especially popular with the working classes. In the heightened, sometimes desperate, atmosphere of Saturday night shopping, haggling and bartering were commonplace, as was pick-pocketing.

This was the uncertain world inhabited by many who still lived in the centre of Queen Victoria's cities. For those who lived in Court 15 it was just around the corner, both in geographical and economic terms. Survival was a matter of providence and hard work (two qualities the Victorians much appreciated), along with a spot of haggling. But the wolf was drawing ever nearer to the door.

TEN

A Brave New World

By 1931 the population of Birmingham had passed one million, and the neighbouring villages and suburbs such as Handsworth, Yardley and Kings Norton, already tied to the city by employment and transport, had officially become part of Greater Birmingham on 1 January 1912. The city's growth was more rapid than any other city in the UK. Only Greater London and Glasgow now had larger populations, and Birmingham would overtake Glasgow in 1947. In general terms the city was beginning to adopt the shape we can still recognise today. There was the old central core (still consisting of pre-1870 housing), surrounded by a middle ring of terraces built between 1870 and 1914, and an outer ring of private and council estates created after the First World War.

The growth of council housing was concentrated in estates often close to the city's outer edges. Kingstanding (begun in 1930 with the purchase of Kettlehouse Farm) was the largest council estate in Europe with 4,802 houses, but even this was only slightly bigger than others at Fox Hollies, Lea Hall, Billesley and Weoley Castle. These new estates swallowed up vast amounts of space, with densities of no more than 12 houses to the acre (the density recommended by the Tudor Walters' Report of 1919) and predictable patterns of cul-de-sacs and crescents.

All these houses had gardens, were fitted with cupboards and dressers and after 1923 had electric light. Heating and cooking were still done on a gas range, with gas heating for a copper. But such amenities did not come cheap. A council house with a parlour could cost 15s 6d a week to rent in the early 1930s, with a non-parlour house costing between 8s and 11s. For those with money to buy, a private house in the suburbs cost around £450. A deposit of £25 could secure the property, with a weekly repayment mortgage of perhaps 13s a week. It was as much a lifestyle that was being bought as a house. Estate agents advertised that such houses were cleaner, healthier and sunnier than life in the inner city and many took the bait. Between 1921 and 1938 there was a drop in population of 22.5 per cent in the central wards and 24.1 in the middle ring, but an increase of 90.8 per cent in the outer ring.

For the back-to-backers of the central area, however, securing a house on an estate was no easy matter. In 1926 the tenant of a non-parlour house had to earn a minimum of £3 10s a week, and £4 a week for a parlour house, at a time when only 16 per cent of the city earned such a wage. But it was the unwaged who found it most difficult. In 1938 Bournville Village Trust commissioned a survey of Birmingham's housing stock as part of its long-term aim to rid the city of its 'tumbledown alleys and monotonous terraces'. The report revealed the surprising statistic that 7.5 per cent of homes in the central wards were now occupied by a single person (compared with a city average of 4.6 per cent). The survey commented:

> ... many of the families of more normal size have migrated to the outskirts in recent years, leaving behind considerable numbers of unattached people. These are mainly elderly, single or widowed, who have no option but to live alone in the house from which their families have moved. For most of them the ideal solution would be properly designed old people's dwellings.

This was certainly true of Court 15, where first George Mitchell and then Constance Wynn lived as sole occupants of their once crowded properties.

What were known as the 'central wards' remained an unpatchable hole in the pocket of the British cities. The Housing Act of 1930 had encouraged the creation of new 'improvement zones', with financial subsidies to local government for re-housing. Court 15, being in Market Hall ward, lay within one of the designated four (later five) Birmingham redevelopment zones, called Bath Row. But the bulldozers were concentrated on the far side of Bristol Street, in the area renamed Lee Bank. Despite the 8,000 houses demolished in these years, many courts remained inhabited. In 1935 there were still 38,773 back-to-backs remaining in the city. In addition the statistics showed there to be 51,794 houses without a separate WC, and 13,650 without a separate water supply. A decade later there were still 29,000 back-to-backs, and 81,000 properties without a bath. One study claimed that 108,000 of the city's houses were in need of either immediate demolition or urgent replacement.

The early 1930s were marked by a concerted campaign against Birmingham's general housing provision. In October 1930 the Anglican and Nonconformist churches in the city launched 'House Improvement Sunday', when preachers across the city condemned slum conditions and over-crowding from the pulpit. One preacher pronounced the city's housing problem unsolved:

> The building activities of the City Council have left the slum problem untouched. The slums still remain a festering sore at the heart of the city's life, breeding disease and degeneracy, and depriving the children born into them of their birthright of a home.

Another added:

> The drab areas in the centre of the city must be cleansed and beautified.
> The 40,000 back-to-back houses must be replaced by modern buildings,
> and the furnished lodgings must no longer disgrace our civilization.

There was still medical justification for concern. The Medical Officer of Health's report for 1931 shows a death-rate of 11.7 per thousand in the city as a whole, compared with a national average of 12.3. But the death-rate in Market Hall ward stood at 15.1. This compares, for example, with 7.9 in Yardley and 9.1 in Acocks Green in the Outer Ring. Deaths through all causes are higher in the central wards, but significantly so from measles, whooping cough, tuberculosis, pneumonia, premature birth and diseases of early infancy.

Those who remained in these time-capsules of neglect did what they could to create their own garden-city. Gwendoline Freeman, who visited the Birmingham courts in the 1930s, was often surprised by a Virginia creeper or lilac bush, or a patch of garden with golden rod, dahlias or Michaelmas daisies, but she added that these often fell victim to children or pets. The yard often accommodated a veritable menagerie of cats and dogs, pigeons, rabbits and hens, the cats (Freeman recalls) being taught to relieve themselves down in the cellar, since there was nowhere in the yard. Canaries, however, seemed to have flown the nest. So common before the war, the vanishing canary was seen as symptomatic of a more general malaise. Writing of the back-to-backs in the Summer Lane area, a reporter from *The Birmingham Post* writes that 'a very few have window-boxes; fewer still have a bird in the window.'

> Some of the panes of glass are broken or cracked, and nearly all the doors
> are half-open. A shut door is a sign either of an extremely cold day or the
> absence of the occupant.

Those who visited and lived in the courts in the early 1930s saw them at their worst. These were hard times, and those in the inner city were hit hard. Unemployment peaked in 1931, when the unemployed in Birmingham (less than the national average) numbered 76,000 (17.7 per cent of the workforce).

It is no coincidence that the recollections of those who endured the hungry Thirties concentrate on food, for life revolved around it. The dole itself was popularly known as 'the treacle stick', because of the tin of treacle sometimes included, and this replaced the usual lard and Daddies' Sauce on the daily bread. Victor Andrews recalls that porridge oats with treacle or salt was another staple meal, or grey dried peas and bacon bits, boiled up and served together. Helen Butcher adds that a pound of 'mixed' from the market—a parsnip, an onion and a carrot—could be supplemented with pearl barley to make a decent stew. For a penny it was possible to buy a bag of broken biscuits or stale cakes from the local coffee shop. Gwen Freeman recalls the occasional appearance of a barrow-boy selling sub-standard bananas. Victor Andrews remembers his childhood treat of condensed milk and a spoonful of cocoa, but also the brimstone and treacle his father concocted as a family panacea. A reporter for *The Birmingham Post* in December 1930 notes the number of eating houses in the Summer Lane area selling 'cheap solid food, hot and cold, from faggots and peas to gob-stoppers …'

Inevitably the pawnshop still offered much needed cash as it had in 1881, the window filled with unredeemed articles, most of them dispensable luxuries like war medals, clocks, engineering tools or ornaments. For those on the bread-line there was at least cheaper shopping to be had in the Bull Ring and its markets. The Rag Market (Rag Alley) operated on Tuesday and Saturday afternoons, selling second-hand and damaged crockery, clothes, furniture and 'knick-knacks'. Leslie Mayell experienced the full wonder of it:

> The market stank mightily; so did many of the people who pushed and shoved, and shouted and swore and haggled. There were piles of rusty nuts and bolts and divers pieces of ironmongery on the floor; second-hand clothes; oldies and antiques; and deal tables with dazzling cheap jewellery. There were several crockery stalls, and invariably a crowd where a big, bull-necked vociferous fellow with a hoarse voice dexterously jangled cups and saucers, plates, dishes, and jerries bedecked with red roses, occasionally smashing on the floor those he couldn't sell. And there was the 'professor', who sold pills, potions and poultices, and kept a huge tapeworm in a glass jar.

Next to the Market Hall stood Woolworth's, which also catered for poorer customers and sold novels for sixpence. In fact, no item cost more than sixpence.

What can we know about the folk in Court 15 at this time ? Ironically, this becomes more tricky than in the Victorian era because of the lack of publicly available records, and the sweeping powers of the Data Protection Act (1998). The names of many of the tenants of Court 15 for this period are available from the electoral rolls, rates books and (most detailed of all) the City of Birmingham Education Census. The latter was compiled by education officers on visits to the court at least twice a year, but their records are closed for 100 years and official permission has to be given for access to this Census. However, under the terms of the Act, none of the names of individuals still alive can be published here unless they have specifically given permission. To compound the difficulties, the lack of census enumerator's books (closed until 2032) prevents us from giving the exact number of residents in the court. Having said that, we have reached a time when living memory can begin to play its part.

One such memory is that of Bette Green (née Mansfield). As a child Bette lived at the back of 65 Hurst Street, the court divided from ours by a high brick wall. She was here in the 1920s, when poverty was rife in the inner city, and it left an indelible impression:

> It was a life of scavenging. If you saw something, you picked it up. Whatever it was it might be of use. We had newspapers hung up at the windows instead of curtains, and there were rats and bugs and God knows what else.

When her parents began one of their heated arguments Bette ran off to the entry of Court 15 and curled up to sleep there. 'There was a pile of old rags or some such. I didn't look too closely.'

There is plenty of other evidence that the standard of living of those still living in the city centre had fallen. An indication of declining economic status in the court can be gleaned from the rates books. Rateable values remain static (at around £6 for the back houses and £16 for the Hurst Street shops and houses) from the 1890s right through to the 1930s. The professions of parents listed in the Education Census

82 Bette Green in one of the bedrooms of Court 15 in 2001, shortly before rebuilding began. Bette lived in the court next to this in the 1920s. The simple lath-and-plaster ceiling was clearly not designed (or expected) to last 180 years.

also seem to indicate a declining standard of living in the hungry '20s and '30s. Robert Howarth at 50 Inge Street is a labourer and window-cleaner, the house occupied in 1935 by George Dowler, deck hand. Alfred Davis, gardener, is at 52 Inge Street from 1932 to 1933. Frank Leaker, car cleaner, lived at 55 Hurst Street from 1928 to 1930, with his four children.

Since the Education Census also records (where known) previous and subsequent addresses we can also get an insight into the difficulties families were facing at this time. One mother, for example (name withheld), brought her three sons and two daughters to 55 Hurst Street in the late 1910s or early 1920s after separation from her husband. Her previous address had been the workhouse. The youngest daughter was sent to Shenley Fields Homes, presumably because her single parent was unable to support all five children. In January 1925 the family moved 'to a room of mansion house, Highfield Road, Moseley'. Two years later (in September 1927) Henry Langston, cycle worker and nurseryman, took his family from the same property to live in a caravan beside the canal off Broad Lane in Alcester Lanes End.

Kelly's Trade Directories allow us to reconstruct the shops occupying the front properties of the court. In 1931 the corner shop at 55 Hurst Street (once owned by the Mitchells) was occupied by James Harold Hurley, confectioner. There had been a sweet shop at 55 Hurst Street from the early years of the 20th century. This was, after all, Birmingham's theatre district, and even if the kids in the court could not afford much in the way of sweets, the patrons of the Hippodrome probably could.

In 1910 the sweet shop was being run by Francis Dibble, but the Hurst Street shops rarely remained in the same hands for long at this time, and by 1930 it was occupied by James Hurley, having gone through a string of different owners (and uses) in the years in between. No doubt the rationing of sweets during the First World War wrecked a number of businesses along the way. But for many in the street the shop at the corner was synonymous with Mr Arthur Bingham, who took over No. 55 in 1934.

Arthur Bingham's bills from the 1960s still have the power to make the mouth water. This was the place to come for sherbert fingers and treacle mints, blackcurrant and aniseed drops, fruit salad and gold butter caramels. There were sour fruits and acid drops, plush nuggets and banana splits, melba fruits and barley sugars. If anything induced the authorities to add fluoride to the water, it was this. But just to show that he was offering a public service as well Mr Bingham also stocked a variety of cough sweets. The latter, it has to be said, was somewhat undermined by the cigarettes behind the counter: Woodbines and Bristols and Capstan Full Strength.

This was the first generation when the names of the manufacturers were becoming as important as the flavour of the product, and shoppers knew the brand names as well as the stockist. So we find Mr Bingham buying his stock from Cadbury's and Rowntree's and Mackintosh, as well as a few firms less well-known today such as Parkes and Lovell's.

After Mr Bingham retired in 1966, the sweet shop was taken over for several years by a Cypriot couple, Maria and Dino Xenides. Birmingham had a long-standing link with the island of Cyprus, especially during the civil war of the 1960s, but Maria's parents had come to the city a generation earlier. They had been running an International Restaurant at the Horse Fair (a five-minute walk from Inge Street) in the 1930s, and then a fish-and-chip shop in Hurst Street. The International Restaurant was practically Birmingham's first encounter with foreign cuisine, and was especially popular with the American-Greek GIs stationed in the city during the Second World War.

83 John Bingham behind the counter of his father's reconstructed sweet shop, now selling sweets once more. The stock is supplied by Sela Traditional Sweet Co., based in Thynne Street, West Bromwich, which has been making a vast range of boiled sweets—sarsaparilla tablets, kali, clove balls, lime juice bricks, rosy apples and the rest—since 1882.

In 1931 the next shop at 57 Hurst Street was occupied by Mrs Hetty Jaggs, bookseller. Hetty took over the shop from Isaac Soper, boot dealer, in 1915 and ran it for the next 17 years. It seems likely that Hetty was selling newspapers as well as books, since the shop remained a newsagent's long after Hetty's departure. In 1936 the lease was taken on by John Edward Hunt. We know somewhat more about Mr Hunt's tenure, though for tragic reasons. In May 1939 a fire broke out in the house, which claimed the life of Marie Josephine Hunt, the tenant's mother, and the resulting inquest has useful information to provide on the internal arrangements in No. 57. Like many of the tenants at that time John Hunt did not live on the premises, but his mother and sister did, and also ran the shop. The first-floor room served as their living-room and the attic as their bedroom, though they undressed for bed in the warmth of the living-room and this (argued the coroner) was probably the cause of the fire. Perhaps a dress had been too close to the fire and continued to smoulder as the two women slept. The fire then found easy passage up the stairs and trapped the women in the attic.

It was a dramatic night on Hurst Street. A passer-by spotted the flames around 6.30 in the morning and an attempt was made to rescue the two women by holding a ladder (hardly long enough) up to the attic. Then a bus was commandeered and parked close to the window to allow the two women to climb across. Hilda Hunt was successfully rescued, but her mother was too 'stout' to squeeze through the small attic window, and there she perished.

One might have expected John Hunt to relinquish his tenure after such a traumatic event, but he did not do so. He remained the owner of the shop until 1945, when it was taken over by Mannie Gorfunkle, who ran it throughout the 1950s and 1960s. By Mannie's day the shop was double-fronted, occupying both 57 and 59 Hurst Street. As for the newsagent himself, the children who grew up on Hurst Street in those years remember him for his sudden and disturbing twitch. But they were taken aside by their parents and told that Mannie had escaped from the clutches of the Nazis in the war. He was therefore perfectly entitled to have a nervous tick.

61 Hurst Street was a baker's shop in the 1930s and stayed in the same hands for more than 50 years, a remarkable case of retailing longevity. Herbert and Ann Read took the shop in 1910 and Ann was still there in the 1960s. Alan Wilkes recalls:

> The back door of the shop opened into Court 15 and the family shared the toilets etc. The shop was called Read's, but everyone knew it as 'the custard shop', because my great-grandfather made egg custards and bread pudding which were sold there. They also sold all types of perishable goods such as bacon, tea and sugar.

Given her trade, it's fitting that Ann Read had a reputation of being a 'tough cookie', with an in-built suspicion of officialdom. Her grand-daughter recalls that during the Second World War Mrs Read was unwilling to entrust her savings to the bank, and kept all her money in the house. Tins that had once held powdered milk were filled instead with half-crowns and deposited in the cellar, while ten-shilling notes were rolled up and hidden up the bedroom chimney. Nor was this the sum of Mrs Read's unusual take on life. Her grand-daughter also recalls her holding séances up on the top floor of No. 61, to the flickering and intoxicating accompaniment of raisins, soaked in brandy and set alight. By such means Mrs Read communicated with a world far away from Court 15.

In 1931 the shop next to the Reads (63 Hurst Street) was occupied by Mrs Ida G. Mantle, milliner. Ida almost rivals the Reads in endurance, her occupation lasting through the two wars from 1914 to 1951. This stands in marked contrast to the earlier years of the century, when the shop passed through six different owners in 13 years. This included a spell of six years when No. 63 was owned by Italians, first as Cesidio Policelli's refreshment rooms and then by the Devoti brothers, who ran it as a confectioner's.

All this may seem to be taking 'micro-history' a little too far, but it is only through examining the details of ownership and occupation that wider patterns emerge. For the retailers of Middle England—and elsewhere, no doubt—it seems that the early years of the 20th century were a time of constant change and

84 Harry Cohen outside his tailor's shop at 53 Inge Street. Harry's daughter, Bette Browne, recalls her father as quite an orthodox Jew. 'He had his hair in ringlets and always wore a hat, and he paid his money to light lamps on the Sabbath.'

85 Alfred Morgan in the living room of 3 House, where he had lived as a child. By the 1930s—the date of the reconstruction—this was the home of the locksmith, George Mitchell, who had lived in the court all his life. George died in the workhouse infirmary in 1936, ending a hundred-year connection between the Mitchell family and Court 15.

short leases. Only in the second decade of the century is there evidence of a more settled situation. The early 1930s (a time of economic hardship) show a further period of instability, but this gives way to a remarkable continuity. The shopkeepers who moved in during or shortly before the Second World War were often still to be seen in the 1960s.

Such a trend can also be seen in the two retail premises in Inge Street. George Mitchell finally relinquished 53 Inge Street on his death in 1936, and in the following April Harry Cohen turned the old lock maker's shop into a tailor's. Harry remained there, through bewildering changes in men's fashion, well into the 1970s. He and Lawrence Levy stand as the alpha and omega of a Jewish connection of 130 years with the court. But whereas the Levys remain a mysterious early presence, the reputation of Harry Cohen spread far and wide. Harry's family arrived as refugees from Russia in the early years of the century, and like many of their compatriots found the Hurst Street area of Birmingham an amenable place to settle. There were still a number of Cohens in Inge Street in the 1930s.

To those who worked in the street Harry Cohen appeared to be a permanent fixture, pressing suits on the steam press in the front window of his shop. Much of his business came from the Hippodrome, and Harry had a collection of signed photographs, the envy of any autograph hunter. Sadly, many of them were pasted to the ceiling of the shop and lost. There was also trade from the professional dancers in 'the pen' at Tony's Ballroom next door. They could be hired for 6d a dance (half of which had to be handed over to the management) and were always, thanks to Harry, immaculately turned out.

It's ironic, given the number of Jewish tailors in and around the court, that both the first and the last of the tailors in Court 15 were not Jews. The earliest we can pick up is Thomas Williams, a Welshman, who was running his tailor's shop at 52 Inge Street in 1851. And at the end of the line was George Saunders, who had the honour of being the last individual to work in Court 15 before its closure in 2002.

George Saunders came from St Kitts in the West Indies. George's father was also a tailor, who went to work for the American forces on the island of Antigua. A strange coincidence this, because George's specialism was also military dress. He took a course in London and ended up making all the trousers for the Queen's Guard, including the leather riding breeches.

George came over to Birmingham in 1958. Like many who arrived from the Caribbean in those years he had no intention of staying indefinitely, but eventually his wife and son came over as well and the family settled down. His initial impression of Birmingham was of the damp and cold 'and a fog so thick that you couldn't see your hand in front of you'. But the weather is something all new arrivals in the city get used to. 'When I first went back to St Kitts 27 years later,' he recalls, 'it was so hot that I got sun-burnt !'

It was not easy to find work in those early days. George got a job in a biscuit factory initially, but it was always his intention to practise the trade he knew best. He worked first at Philip Collier's, the tailor's, before setting up in business on his own in Bordesley Green. He moved into 61-63 Hurst Street in 1975, taking over the shop from a TV rental firm, and hoping to get work from the Hippodrome next door, but by then they had their own tailors.

Like many tailors before him, George Saunders built up his reputation, and his customer base, by word of mouth. Assisted by his son, George made, mended and altered, and his shop was an Aladdin's Cave of suits, trousers and jackets. Using only the best quality cloth, George delighted in transforming his customer into the best dressed man in town.

The final retail property—52 Inge Street—did not remain so for long. There is a sequence of Jewish proprietors from 1912, but no indication in the trade directories of the nature of their businesses. Mrs Rebecca Edelstein took over the property in 1924, in whose house (according to the electoral roll for October 1931) also lived Minnie

86 Court 15 in 2004. The three back houses in the court have been reconstructed to reflect life in the 1840s, 1880s and 1930s, while George Saunders' tailoring business occupies a fourth. The three front houses in Inge Street are now used as short lets, providing visitors to the city with a novel alternative to the usual hotel room. The first occupants were Brian and Pauline Meakin, who were the last residents to leave the court back in 1967.

Shalansky. Before them 52 Inge Street had been occupied by Goodman Cohen, whose granddaughter, Eva, attended the Hebrew School in Hurst Street.

Rebecca Edelstein had left the court by February 1932. Once it was abandoned as a shop 52 Inge Street saw a rapid turnover in tenants, a feature of most city centre properties by this time. The Education Census picks up the following brief and varied tenancies:

> Alfred Davis, gardener, from April 1932 to April 1933
> Maurice Bishop, metal roller, from May 1933 to June 1934
> Bunny Bunroe, astrologer, from June 1934
> (Name withheld), waiter, from June 1935 to April 1936
> Evans (no first name given), from May 1936

87 Rose Bingham and her mother, Florence Wiggett, outside the sweet shop at 55 Hurst Street in 1936. Rose ran the shop while Arthur Bingham had a cabinet making business elsewhere in the city. The family owned the shop from 1934 until 1966, though they only lived upstairs until 1941.

Like No. 52 the adjacent house at 50 Inge Street had a number of Jewish occupiers. The Education Census tells us that Samuel Altman lived there until November 1921, with two children (Leria and Phyllis) who also attended the Hebrew School. There was another Jewish occupant (Israel Simons, a tailor) until September 1928, when he left for America. A family by the name of Josephs moved into 3 House in April 1937.

The time-honoured use of the yard itself for manufacturing purposes comes to an end with Frederick Horton, who ran his glazier's business at the back of 53 Inge Street (presumably 3 House) from 1910 to 1920.

It is a distinctively different aspect of the court from the 1930s onward that it was no longer entirely residential. Harold and Annie Hurley did not live in Hurst Street, but in Trafalgar Road, Moseley, using No. 55 only as a lock-up shop. In 1942 Arthur Bingham moved his family to Solihull and rented the shop to his brother-in-law, Robert Wiggett, who lived upstairs with his wife and three children. One of these children, Robert Wiggett, describes the complex way the house had been divided into a retail and domestic area:

> Entry into 55 Hurst Street was by a small passageway to a door, which
> led up a flight of stairs to a living area. The room consisted of two

windows, one bay window overlooking Inge Street, and another on Hurst Street, a small fireplace and a stove in the corner. A second flight of stairs led to a large bedroom, which we all slept in.

Rooms in 59 and 63 Hurst Street were similarly rented out by the retailers. Brian Meakin, a former resident, remarks that in the 1960s non-resident shopkeepers were renting out their upstairs rooms to lodgers, and this was clearly the case as far back as the 1930s. Such temporary residents will rarely appear on the electoral roll or on the Education Census. The education officers, however, were careful to note the presence of lodgers in a house occupied by children. Lodgers are mentioned twice at 2 House during the 1910s and 1920s, and the upper floor(s) of 55 Hurst Street were occupied by George Hulton, a tramway man, and his two children in 1925. No fewer than five tenants are noted at 57 Hurst Street during the 1930s, including the intriguing Madame Parker, palmist. They too probably occupied the upstairs rooms. All these tenants paid their weekly 'rent', of course, to the occupiers of the house, and the two or three shillings involved would noticeably supplement the income of the family downstairs. They provided an additional form of security for the shopkeepers too. There were also temporary traders. Harry Cohen found space in his shop for a local caricaturist, Doug Roberts, to ply his trade, and proudly displayed a caricature of himself in the window of the shop.

The back houses were more likely to accommodate longer-term residents. The Wynn family who lived at 1 House, for example, seemed to be permanent fixtures. Sarah Wynn appears on the 1901 census as a widow and a laundress working from home. She and five of her six children listed there—James, Emma, Florence, Constance and Edith—still appear in the voters' list for 1931. Constance Wynn, probably born and certainly raised in Court 15, was one of the last to move out in 1967.

And so we come to the final act of a drama that has run for 200 years. During the 1950s and 1960s Birmingham pursued a redevelopment policy that was fast and furious, and those still living in the Central Redevelopment Areas were moved out and their old houses demolished. The housing inspectors called the inhabitants CRAs, and condemned their homes (and often their lifestyles) with the stroke of pen. The few properties that remained provided temporary accommodation for those queueing for a council house. One such family were the Meakins. Brian Meakin was a scaffolder by trade, and living with his wife, Pauline, in a flat on Hagley Road. But fate intervened to take them to Court 15, as Brian records:

> I had a fall, which put me out of work, and we had to look for cheaper accommodation. The rent at 2 Back 52 Inge Street was 11s 6d a week. Some turned their nose up at back-to-backs, but it was a little palace

to us. We had the three rooms—living room, bedroom and attic—and a toilet out in the yard. We couldn't use the brewhouse, though. So we used the tin lizzie or went to Kent Street baths instead.

By the time they left the court in 1965 the Meakins were a family of four, and their younger daughter, Debbie, had the honour of being the last baby to be born in the court. She stands at the end of a line that began with Thomas Mitchell, 115 years before.

By 1964 only four of the properties—50 Inge Street and the three back houses—were still being lived in, and by 1966 that number had been reduced to two. Peter and Barbara Morgan were living at 50 Inge Street, and Constance Wynn was still in 1 House, as she had been in 1901. These were then the last residential occupants of the court. No one is listed in the electoral roll for October 1967. The emptying of Court 15 can be seen in the context of a mass migration from the central wards in general as clearance schemes progressed. Between 1951 and 1961 something like 36,000 people (or 39.2 per cent) left the area, and a further 29,000 (or 25.9 per cent) between 1961 and 1966.

88 Brian and Pauline Meakin in the living room of what had once been their home, the middle house of the court. In the 1960s their rent was 11s 6d a week. 'People called them slums,' comments Brian, 'but we didn't look at them as slums. It was a little palace to us. We all have good memories of Court 15, but particularly of the people there. Everyone was friendly and willing to share whatever they had.'

After 1966 Court 15 was used entirely for retail, and the back houses, where so many had lived and died over the 130 years of their residential life, became storage areas. The Asian-owned taxi firm and kebab house which vacated the properties in Inge Street in 2002 seem to show little continuity with the life that preceded them. But the lines that history draws are always blurred. Hurst Street remains the multi-cultural and international area it had been in the 1840s. In the 1970s there were still a number of Jewish tailors in the street and another from the Caribbean was shortly to be setting up in business. Other properties included Italian restaurants, an Indian restaurant and a kebab house. In addition, there was a Dutch watch repairer at 62 Hurst Street and Norwegian shipping agents at 109 Hurst Street. Back in 1959 an Irish club—the Shamrock—took over the top floor of the building next door to the Hippodrome. Today there is a Thai restaurant too, and Birmingham's Chinatown is just around the corner.

Today those leaving the Hippodrome at the end of the show are considerably better-heeled than the crowd who once trooped out of the Tivoli, and the music on offer at the street's clubs is rather different from what the old dance-halls provided. Gone are the coalman, the lamplighter and the nightsoilman who once shuffled down the entry into Court 15. The footsteps now are of short-breakers and tourists and schoolchildren. But still the old court looks on. Footfalls echo in the memory, said T. S. Eliot, and time past and time present are united.

Bibliography

All titles published Birmingham unless otherwise stated.

Chapter 1: A Street in History

John Burnett, *A Social History of Housing 1815-1985* (2nd edn London, 1986)

George Holyoake, *Sixty Years of an Agitator's Life* (1900)

John S. Nettlefold, *A Housing Policy* (1905)

L.W. Darra Mair, 'Report on Back-to-Back Houses', *Parliamentary Papers* XXXVII (1910)

Report of the Artisans' Dwellings Committee (1884)

Chapter 2: A Maximum of Rent for a Minimum of Outlay

Maxine Berg, *The Age of Manufactures 1700-1820* (London, 1994)

Asa Briggs, *A Social History of England* (Harmondsworth, 1994)

Lucy Caffyn, *Workers' Housing in West Yorkshire 1750-1920*, Royal Commission on the Historical Monuments of England, HMSO, 1986

C.W. Chalklin, *The Provincial Towns of Georgian England. A Study of the Building Process 1740-1820* (Montreal, 1974)

M.W. Beresford, 'The Back-to-Back House in Leeds 1878-1937' in Stanley D. Chapman (ed.), *The History of Working-Class Housing* (Newton Abbot, 1971)

Phil Chapple, *The Industrialisation of Britain 1780-1914* (London, 1999)

N.F.R. Crafts, *British Industrial Growth during the Industrial Revolution* (Oxford, 1985)

Alasdair Clayre (ed.), *Nature and Industrialisation* (Oxford, 1977)

John Alfred Langford, *A Century of Birmingham Life or Chronicle of Local Events from 1741 to 1841* (1868)

William F. Laughlan (ed.), *First Impressions of England and its People: Hugh Miller* (Hawick, 1983)

Trevor May (ed.), *An Economic and Social History of Britain 1760-1990* (Harlow, 1995)

Kenneth Morgan, *The Birth of Industrial Britain. Economic Change 1750-1850* (London, 1999)

Barrie Trinder, *The Making of the Industrial Landscape* (London, 1997)

Chapter 3: Living at the Bottom of Wells

Chris Aspin, *The First Industrial Society. Lancashire 1750-1850* (Preston, 1995)

J.T. Bunce, *History of the Corporation of Birmingham*, Vol. II (1885)

Birmingham Corporation, *Report of the Artizans' Dwellings Committee* (1984)

Stanley D. Chapman (ed.), *The History of Working-Class Housing (*Newton Abbot, 1971)

Carl Chinn, *Homes for People. Council Housing and Urban Renewal in Birmingham 1849-1999* (Studley, Warwickshire, 1999)

M.J. Daunton, *House and Home in the Victorian City. Working-Class Housing 1850-1914* (London, 1983)

S. Martin Gaskell, *Building Control. National Legislation and the Introduction of Local Bye-laws in Victorian England* (London, 1983)

Enid Gauldie, *Cruel Habitations. A History of Working-Class Housing 1780-1918* (London, 1974)

David Rubinstein, *Victorian Homes* (Newton Abbot, 1974)

Chris Upton, *A History of Birmingham* (Chichester, 1993)

Anthony S. Wohl, *Endangered Lives. Public Health in Victorian Britain* (London, 1983)

Chapter 4: Running to Stand Still

Bournville Village Trust, *When We Build Again* (London, 1941)

John Burnett, *A Social History of Housing* (2nd edn 1986)

Gordon E. Chery, *Birmingham. A Study in Geography, History and Planning* (Chichester, 1994)

Eric Hopkins, *Industrialisation and Society. A Social History 1830-1951* (London, 2000)

Eric Hopkins, *Birmingham. The Making of the Second City 1850-1939* (Stroud, 2001)

Robert Roberts, *The Classic Slum. Salford Life in the First Quarter of the Century* (Manchester, 1971)

John Stevenson, 'The Jerusalem that Failed? The Rebuilding of Post-War Britain' in Terry Gourvish and Alan O'Day (eds), *Britain since 1945* (London, 1991)

Chapter 5: Life for Rent: Living in the Back-to-Backs

Victor J. Andrews, *Patched Parts* (1981)

Helen Butcher, *The Treacle Stick* (1999)

City of Birmingham, *Report on Survey of Housing Conditions* (1929)

Gwendolen Freeman, *The Houses Behind* (1947)

Syd Garrett, *I Remember ... Tales of Old Ladywood* (n.d.)

M. Green, *Brum Memories* (n.d.)

Dennis Harding, *From the Shadow of Poverty* (2002)

Peter James and Richard Sadler, *Homes Fit for Heroes. The Photographs of Bill Brandt 1939-1943* (2004)

Leslie Mayell, *More Memories of Birmingham* (1982)

Keith Wilson, '2 / 153 Great Hampton Row, Birmingham', *Birmingham Historian*, 12, pp.37-39

Correspondence/reminiscence from Oliver Burns, Tom Foster, Sheila Gordon, Stephanie Graham, Betty Green, Iris Hackett, Violet Henley, Paul Lawrence, Mrs J. Mead, William Ridley, Maurice Spence, Bob Tebbett, Jean Whitehead

Chapter 6: The Big Yard

J.T. Bunce, *History of the Corporation of Birmingham*, Vol. II (1885)

Helen Butcher, *The Treacle Stick* (1999)

M.J. Daunton, *House and Home in the Victorian City. Working-Class Housing 1850-1914* (London, 1983)

Syd Garrett, *I Remember ... Tales of Old Ladywood* (n. d.)

Enid Gauldie, *Cruel Habitations. A History of Working-Class Housing 1780-1918* (London, 1974)

George Holyoake, *Sixty Years of an Agitator's Life* (1900)

Robert Rawlinson, *Report to the General Board of* Health (London, 1849)

C.A. Vince, *History of the Corporation of Birmingham*, Vol. III (1902)

E. Cumming Walters, *Scenes in Slum-Land* (1901)

Correspondence / reminiscence from Linda Denny, Mr T.D. Foster, Allan J. Gripton, Sheila Gordon, Mrs J. Mead, Maggie Rider, Maurice Spence, Bob Tebbett and Jean Whitehead.

Chapter 7: The Metropolis of the Midlands

John Thackeray Bunce, *History of the Corporation of Birmingham*, Vol. 1 (1878)

Simon Buteux, *Beneath the Bull Ring. The Archaeology of Life and Death in Early Birmingham* (Studley, Warwickshire, 2003)

David Cannadine, *Lords and Landlords. The Aristocracy and the Towns 1774-1967* (Leicester, 1980)

C.W. Chalklin, *The Provincial Towns of Georgian England. A Study of the Building Process 1740-1820* (Montreal, 1974)

Conrad Gill, *History of Birmingham*, Vol. 1 (London, 1952)

Eric Hopkins, *Birmingham. The First Manufacturing Town in the World 1760-1840* (London, 1989)

Doreen Hopwood and Margaret Dilloway, *Bella Brum. A History of Birmingham's Italian Community* (1996)

Chris Upton, *A History of Birmingham* (Chichester, 1993)

Index

compiled by Peter Ellis

Note: Page numbers in *italics* refer to illustrations and captions.
All street names and other locales are in Birmingham

Samuel and Nathaniel Buck's south-west prospect of Birmingham (1731). The Bucks took as their vantage point a position close to what is now the junction of Inge Street and Hurst Street, the future location of Court 15. Digbeth and Deritend is on the far right of the view. At its highest point (by St Philip's church) the town was 453 feet above sea level, a considerable challenge to the canal engineers a generation later. (See also front endpaper.)